# VISION/VISUAL PERCEPTION

*An Annotated Bibliography*

Compiled by
Sam Weintraub and
Robert J. Cowan

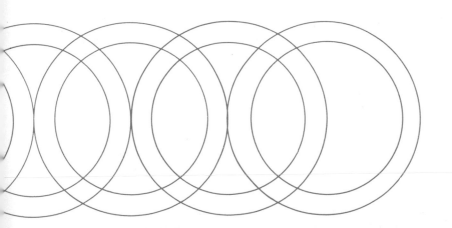

# VISION/VISUAL PERCEPTION

*An Annotated Bibliography*

*1982 Edition*
Compiled by
Sam Weintraub and
Robert J. Cowan
State University of New York at Buffalo

Published by the
INTERNATIONAL READING ASSOCIATION
800 Barksdale Road    Newark, Delaware 19711

# INTERNATIONAL READING ASSOCIATION

Copyright 1982 by the
International Reading Association, Inc.

**Library of Congress Cataloging in Publication Data**

Weintraub, Sam, 1927-
  Vision/visual perception.

  1. Perceptual-motor learning—Abstracts.
2. Visually handicapped—Abstracts. 3. Visual
perception—Abstracts. 4. Reading—Abstracts.
I. Cowan, Robert J. II. Title.
LB1067.W45  1982      016.37191'1      82-7205
ISBN 0-87207-339-4              AACR2

ii

# Contents

# Introduction

**This research bibliography** is an updating and modification of *Vision-Visual Discrimination* published in 1973. It contains the studies and research related articles published since then. For the 1973 edition, materials were identified by the then Eric Clearinghouse for Reading, Eric/Crier. The newer entries come from the annual summaries of research in reading published by IRA. Annotations and/or abstracts have not been rewritten for this bibliography; they appear as found in the original Eric/Crier system or in the annual summaries.

In the decade since the publication of the first bibliography, a considerable amount of new research has appeared in the area of visual discrimination. However, because of space and cost considerations, it became necessary to limit the number of entries. Therefore, the sections on perceptual motor development and on eye movements have been deleted in the 1982 edition. Also, Part 2, Visual Perception, is a selective listing only. In particular, research dealing with adults has been deleted so that the emphasis is on research in visual perception of preschool and school age children. Individuals wishing more recent information on eye movement research and perceptual motor programs are referred to the annual summaries of research in reading.

The first large category, Vision, is divided into two subgroups: 1)Visually Handicapped and 2) Visual Acuity and Efficiency. This section might be of use to individuals in the field of optometry and ophthalmology as well as to school personnel interested in the relationship of visual acuity and efficiency to learning to read or to reading problems. Persons who work with the blind or visually impaired also would find entries of interest in this section.

The Visual Perception category contains a wide assortment of diversified research on different topics loosely related to visual perception. Included under that heading are articles dealing with visual training programs, visual memory, visual discrimination, and visual perceptual testing. This category would probably be of value to individuals making curricular decisions, particularly ones related to kindergarten readiness, beginning reading programs, and remedial reading instruction.

In the 1973 edition of this bibliography, some concerns were raised about the research in the area of visual perception. Interestingly, the area remains one still fraught with considerable controversy. Rather than clarify issues, the research has frequently added fuel to the fire. As noted in the introduction to the 1973 publication, the problem is often one of lack of rigor in design such as poor controls or questionable instrumentation. The addition of research on learning disabilities has added to the confusion. The assessment instruments used are sometimes of questionable validity. For these and other reasons, the consumer of the literature in this area must continue to read with a particularly critical eye and must carefully evaluate.

The call for replication research is still an urgent need. We need to do far more testing before implementing a program. Too frequently the "proof" of a program's effectiveness is demonstrated solely by growth on a standardized instrument. Not only is the assessment of that growth sometimes questionable, but other dimensions of a program's effect on users are sometimes overlooked. Little gain is made in implementing a program which may indicate that test scores are raised when, at the same time, we may be teaching children some negative attitudes and/or incorrect concepts through its use.

In summary, this bibliography contains a broad spectrum of articles, primarily research or reviews of research, all dealing with some aspect of vision. Within the bibliography the reader will find controversial and contradictory viewpoints and evidence. It is hoped that the reader who uses this bibliography will go to the original source and read critically and reflect thoughtfully on what is found there.

SW<br>
RJC

# Part 1
# Vision

**This section of the bibliography** has been divided into two subcategories. Section 1 has materials in it that are related to the reading of blind and partially sighted individuals. The second section contains articles that discuss visual acuity and efficiency as they relate to reading. Included in this latter category are such topics as aniseikonia, accommodation and convergence, suppression, and binocular coordination.

## Section 1. The Visually Handicapped

BATEMAN, BARBARA D. *Reading and psycholinguistic processes of partially seeing children.* CEC Research Monograph No. 5. Washington, D.C.: National Education Association, Council for Exceptional Children, 1963.
Makes a comparison of the test performance of 131 pupils in grades 1 through 4 enrolled in 20 classes of partially seeing pupils, with the norms of the tests.

BERGER, ALLEN. Evaluation of an informal reading inventory for the blind. In. G. B. Schick and M. M. May (Eds.), *The Psychology of Reading Behavior.* Yearbook of the National Reading Conference, 18, 1969, 200-206.
Compares a Braille Informal Reading Inventory, constructed by the author, to reading comprehension and word meaning scores on standardized Braille achievement tests for 147 blind children (86 boys and 61 girls).

BERLA, EDWARD P., & BUTTERFIELD, LAWRENCE H., JR. Tactile political maps: two experimental designs. *Visual Impairment and Blindness,* June 1977, 71, 262-267.
Investigates the ability and speed of seventy-two Braille readers in grades 4-12 to locate and trace shapes on three types of tactile political maps. Two experimental maps, one with broad raised boundary lines

and one with broad incised boundary lines, were each tested against a typical map with thin raised lines (control map). All three types of maps were otherwise identical, consisting of six states placed randomly among other boundary lines. Performance on the broad raised line map was superior to that on the control map, but performance on the broad incised line map was not.

CARPENTER, PATRICIA A., & EISENBERG, PETER. Mental rotation and the frame of reference in blind and sighted individuals. *Perception and Psychophysics,* February 1978, *23,* 117-124.
Investigates the ability of congenitally blind and blindfolded, sighted students to mentally rotate in space with a haptic letter judgment task. In a series of 4 experiments, blind and sighted subjects were presented a letter in some orientation between 0° and 300° from upright, and they were timed while they judged whether it was a normal or mirror-image letter. Both groups had an increasing response time with the stimulus's departure from upright; this result was interpreted as reflecting the process of rotation. Experiment 1 indicated that 12 congenitally blind high school students could mentally rotate on a non-visual representation. Experiments 2 and 3 duplicated the blind subjects' findings, using 23 sighted college students first with a visual, then with a haptic letter presentation. Results suggest that mental rotation can operate on a spatial representation that does not have any specifically visual components. Experiment 4 indicated that for the sighted subjects in the haptic task, the orientation of the letter is coded with respect to the position of the hand. Sighted subjects may code the orientation of the letter and then either translate the code into a visual representation or use of a spatial representation that is not specifically visual.

CATON, HILDA. A primary reading program for beginning Braille readers. *Journal of Visual Impairment and Blindness,* October 1979, *73,* 309-313.
Reviews the research in the area of Braille reading, tactual perception, concept development in blind children and current practices in teaching reading in order to compile a set of specifications for a Braille reading series. These specifications provide guidelines for the selection of both appropriate vocabulary and teaching methodology for blind readers.

CLINE, CAROL S., & CARDINALE, JOHN. Braille reading: a review of research. *Education of the Visually Handicapped,* March 1971, *3,* 7-10.
Summarizes nine research articles to provide historical perspective of trends leading up to and culminating in the present challenge to

teachers of visually handicapped as to their approaches to Braille reading.

DAUGHERTY, KATHRYN M. Monterey learning systems: improving academic achievement of visually impaired learners. *Visual Impairment and Blindness,* September 1977, *71,* 298-301.
Reports the effects of the Pittsburg Public Schools 1975-1976 project involving the use of the *Monterey Learning Systems Reading and Mathematics Program* to enhance the academic competencies of the visually impaired. These highly individualized programs, which include a diagnostic component and much accountability, served as a 5-month supplement to the schooling of twenty-nine visually impaired students. Pre- and posttests on the *Gilmore Oral Reading Test* (Form C) yielded average gains of just over one year in decoding and just under one year in comprehension. Gains of similar magnitude were made in math.

FOULKE, EMERSON. Increasing the Braille reading rate. *Journal of Visual Impairment and Blindness,* October 1979, *73,* 318-323.
Examines possibilities for increasing the reading rate of Braille readers: 1) to change the perceptual ability of the Braille reader; 2) to change the manner in which the Braille characters are displayed; and 3) to change the code. Reviews the related literature.

FOULKE, EMERSON. Investigative approaches to the study of Braille reading. *Journal of Visual Impairment and Blindness,* October 1979, *73,* 298-308.
Reviews research studies related to three general approaches to the study of Braille reading. In the first group, studies are summarized which deal with the observation and description of Braille reading behavior and comparisons of fast and slow readers. The second set of studies was concerned with determining the legibility of Braille characters and readability of words composed of Braille characters. The third group of studies related to the manner in which Braille characters are displayed in order to observe their effects on reading behavior. This literature review makes suggestions for further research.

FOULKE, EMERSON. Non-visual communication: IX. Reading by touch (continued). *Education of the Visually Handicapped,* December 1970, *2,* 122-124.
Reviews four studies on the comparison of visual reading as compared with touch reading with regard to the word rate achieved.

FOULKE, EMERSON. Non-visual communication: X. Reading by touch (continued). *Education of the Visually Handicapped,* March 1971, *3,* 25-28.

Reviews 10 research studies done with Braille readers to alleviate the slow rate of their reading.

GOODRICH, GREGORY L.; BENNETT, RICHARD R.; DE L'AUNE, WILLIAM R.; LAUER, HARVEY; & MOWINSKI, LEONARD. Kurzweil reading machine: a partial evaluation of its optical character recognition error rate. *Journal of Visual Impairment and Blindness,* December 1979, *73,* 389-399.

Evaluates the optical character recognition (OCR) of the Kurzweil Reading Machines (KRM) by assessing OCR error rate using three different type styles and five means of producing copy; by assessing the effect of the KRM's learning feature; by classifying the type of OCR errors made by type style and method of materials production; by assessing inter-machine reliability among three KRMs, and developing a general protocol to be used to evaluate OCR error rates with subsequent generation KRMs and other synthetic-speech reading machines. Results indicated that the KRMs have different error rates depending upon the means of copy production and the type style; there was a significant interaction between copy method and type style. Error rates varied between less than one percent to more than 20%. In general, as the quality of the material decreases, the number of errors made by the machines increased. As the error rate increases, the user experienced greater difficulty in understanding the spoken output.

GOODRICH, GREGORY L.; MEHR, EDWIN B.; QUILLMAN, ROBERT D.; SHAW, HELEN K.; & WILEY, J. KENNETH. Training and practice effects in performance with low-vision aids: a preliminary study. *American Journal of Optometry and Physiological Optics,* May 1977, *54,* 312-318.

Measures reading speed and duration for 24 low-vision veterans assigned to 1 of 2 training groups for 10 days. One group (N= 12) receiving reading training used a closed-circuit television (CCTV); the other (N=12) learned to use other optical aids. Initial measures indicated no significant difference between the 2 groups in reading speed. Both groups showed statistically significant increases from day 1 to day 10. On the final day, the CCTV group was reading significantly faster than the optical aid group. Improvements occurred by steplike increases and plateaus. Neither far nor near visual acuity was a significant predictor of reading performance. Because the data showed large intrasubject variability and increases in reading performance, the authors recommend caution in rejecting low-vision aids on the basis of a single trial.

HALL, AMANDA, & RODABAUGH, BARBARA. Development of a pre-reading concept program for visually handicapped children. *Journal of Visual Impairment and Blindness,* September 1979, *73,* 257-263.

Describes the development and formative evaluation of an individualized program for teaching concepts to visually handicapped children at a pre-reading level. The program, which emphasized concrete multisensory experiences and appropriate language in conjunction with the manipulative tasks, was field tested with 11 teachers and 20 students at various departmental levels. Evaluative data were collected by means of progress logs submitted by the teachers and teacher interviews. Progress log data revealed that time needed to teach each lesson was within reasonable limits. Teachers rated two-thirds of the lessons to be appropriately difficult. Pretest scores yielded data on the logical sequencing of lessons. Interviews with teachers revealed that program strengths included ease of use, high interest level, and choice of concepts.

HAMPSHIRE, BARRY E. Tactile and visual reading. *The New Outlook for the Blind*, April 1975, *69*, 145-155.
Reviews the literature on reading, including information processing aspects, the role of the sensory register, and short-term and long-term memory to compare processes involved in visual and tactile reading.

HARLEY, RANDALL K., & RAWLS, RACHEL. Comparison of several approaches for teaching Braille reading to blind children. *Education of the Visually Handicapped,* May 1970, *2*, 47-51.
Determines the effectiveness of various approaches to teaching of beginning reading to blind children, using 39 beginning Braille readers with mean IQ 82.667.

KELLEHER, DENNIS K. A pilot study to determine the effect of the bioptic telescope on young vision patients' attitude and achievement. *American Journal of Optometry and Physiological Optics,* March 1974, *51,* 198-205.
Determines the effect of bioptic telescopic spectacles on attitude and achievement in reading, spelling, and arithmetic for 5 low vision subjects.

KIKUCHI, TADASHI; YAMASHITA, YUKIO; SAGAWA, KEN; & WAKE, TENJI. An analysis of tactile letter confusions. *Perception & Psychophysics,* October 1979, *26,* 295-301.
Describes the kinds of information four adult blind persons (two congenitally and two adventitiously) used in recognizing tactile letters presented on their backs. A further purpose was to investigate the nature of the mutual interaction of multiple point stimulators when blind subjects try to recognize tactile letters. In the experiment, 26 letters of the alphabet were presented at random while the subject pressed back against a tactile matrix and was asked to identify the letter. After 20 blocks of the experiment the performances tended to

increase up to about 90%, although there were variations in performance. The two adventitiously blind subjects did not show any notable improvement in performance. Their identification remained at about 40%, possibly because of fewer trials before the experiment began. The identification performance of even the congenitally blind subjects deteriorated after they had been away from the experimental situation for a length of time. The letter *I* was easiest to identify and *G* the most difficult.

KIRSCHNER, CONRINNE, PETERSON, RICHARD, & SUHR, CAROL. Trends in school enrollment and reading methods among legally blind school children, 1963-1978 (Statistical Brief #6). *Journal of Visual Impairment and Blindness*, November 1979, *73,* 373-375, 377, 379.
Reports and analyzes data gathered annually by the American Printing House for the Blind from records submitted by residential and non-residential schools. Specifically, data are compiled which relate to the social aspects of blindness, including the reading methods employed and the types of school situations. Trends showed a rise in total number of legally blind children from 1963 to 1978 (17,090 to 29,403). By 1978, 24% of the legally blind school children were enrolled in residential schools (down from 45% in 1963). The proportion of children in ungraded programs in both residential and non-residential settings has increased. There appeared to be a sharp decline in the percentage of legally blind students who use Braille and an increase in those classified as using neither Braille nor large type, relying instead on regular print, recorded materials, sighted readers, or combinations of the preceding.

KLEINSTEIN, ROBERT N. Reading with a 10X telescope. *Journal of Optometry and Physiological Optics*, October 1978, *55,* 732-734.
Presents a case report describing use of a 10X Selsi telescope with a + 3.50D reading cap with a 10-year old partially sighted, one-eyed patient with 10/200 distance acuity and no experience in using an optical aid. With the telescope and cap, the patient could read 20/40 at 28 cm. To permit the patient use of both hands to hold the device, or to hold the device and write, a reading easel was prepared to hold the material upright and a high intensity lamp was used for illumination control. The light improved the contrast of the material and the stand eliminated some of the fatigue. The researcher believed the solution to be unique and reported one successful replication.

LEWIS, PAUL J., & MARON, SHELDON. Teachers' evaluation for low vision needs: an instrument for assessing educational visual functioning. *Education of the Visually Handicapped*, Fall 1977, *9,* 65-71.
Describes the development and field testing to determine reliability of an instrument designed to assist in the prescription of appropriate

print size for partially sighted students. In a test/retest situation, 54 legally blind and partially sighted students (reading levels 1 through 6) in 7 large Florida school districts were measured for rate and word recognition on 6-paragraph reading selections, controlled for difficulty and with each paragraph (except the last) printed in successively smaller type size. For all sizes of type included, coefficients ranged from .74 to .88 for total reading errors and between .69 to .91 for reading rate between pretest and posttest. There was also evidence that print size between 18 and 10 points had little effect on students' reading speed or number of word recognition errors.

LOGAR, NOEL D. A marble used as a low-vision reading aid: a case report. *American Journal of Optometry and Physiological Optics*, December 1977, *54*, 849-851.
Describes attempts to provide suitable optical devices for a low-vision, 39-year-old male. The patient's unaided visual acuity in the left eye was 20/400 and was not improved by refraction; the right eye had only light perception. At age 8, the patient discovered he could accomplish near-point reading using an ordinary glass marble as a magnifier. The marble permitted reading of smaller type and for long periods of time—up to 6 hours a day. Rate improvement with the marble was from 55 to 84 words per minute on a standardized reading exercise. It was found that the patient could better be assisted with a commercially available magnifier of less dioptric power. While reading speed did not significantly improve with the 3-lens optical aid, the patient reported ease of use and clarity of print.

LORIMER, JOHN, & TOBIN, MICHAEL J. Experiments with modifier Grade 2 Braille codes to determine their effect on reading speed. *Journal of Visual Impairment and Blindness*, October 1979, *73*, 324-328.
Describes four experiments in which Standard English Braille is compared with three "reduced" codes and one "expanded" code to determine effects on adult blind subjects' speed of reading. Subjects were randomly assigned to one of four groups and asked to read two prose passages, one in Standard English Grade Two Braille, and the other in a modified code. In Experiments Three and Four, subjects answered comprehension questions. For Experiment One, the reduced code of contractions and the conditions of no pre-practice with the code may have contributed to Standard Braille texts being read significantly more rapidly. In Experiment Four, expansion of the code led to a significantly superior mean rate on the Standard Braille test. Experiments Two and Three produced no significant differences. The authors indicated that space saving and ease of learning are other criteria that need to be considered when Braille is modified.

LOWENFELD, BERTHOLD; ABEL, GEORGIE LEE; & HATLEN, PHILIP H. *Blind children learn to read.* Springfield, Illinois: Charles C. Thomas, 1969.

Explores the present status of Braille reading in local classes and residential schools for blind children and determines, on the basis of 337 questionnaires and scores on two reading tests of 100 fourth and eighth graders, the characteristics of efficient readers and effective instructional techniques.

MANGOLD, SALLY S. Tactile perception and Braille letter recognition: effects of developmental teaching. *Journal of Visual Impairment and Blindness,* September 1978, *72,* 259-266.

Studies the extent to which a developmental program of tactile perception and Braille letter recognition affected the three most frequent errors in Braille reading: tactile perception, Braille letter recognition, and scrubbing and backtracking behaviors. Thirty blind Braille users, aged 5-15, were matched according to date of birth, visual acuity, extent of braille use, beginning or remedial school placement (public or residential), and pretest scores. The treatment condition consisted of administration of 227 worksheets. The ten pretest measures served as a posttest and as a 2-month follow-up to determine the degree of maintenance of experimental effects. While analysis of pretest data established equivalency of groups, the analysis of the posttest data revealed a highly significant difference in favor of the experimental group on all ten tests. The experimental subjects demonstrated significantly less scrubbing and backtracking and made fewer errors in letter recognition.

MARMOLIN, HANS; NILSSON, LARS-GORAN; & SMEDSHAMMAR, HANS. The mediated reading process of the partially sighted. *Visible Language,* 1979, *13*(2), 168-183.

Proposes and tests a reading model for the partially sighted. Reading rates of 41 good, average, and poor partially sighted readers were compared for isolated letters, words, sentences and paragraphs. For all groups the reading of letters was slower than the reading of words, sentences, and paragraphs. The sentence reading of poor readers was slower than their word reading, while the opposite was true for good readers. Results suggested that poor readers could not utilize semantic content and follow a mediated, letter by letter model. Further breakdown of subjects into finer medical categories was attempted as was an evaluation of training procedures.

MARTIN, CLESSEN J., & BASSIN, CAROLYN B. Effects of two telegraphic deletion schemes on the reading behavior of Braille readers. *Journal of Special Education,* Summer 1977, *11,* 233-241.

Reports a programmatic research effort which has attempted to develop and evaluate a telegraphic writing style to increase the efficiency of Braille reading. Three different types of literature (science, fiction, and news) were reduced by 20 percent, then by 40 percent of their words through either a subjective or a computerized frequency method. Reading performance of 36 legally blind Braille readers in grades 8 to 12 was assessed by a multiple choice comprehension test and by measures of reading rate and time. No significant differences in comprehension were obtained either as a function of the type of deletion scheme or rate of deletion. There was evidence of slower reading rates among children reading the 40 percent telegraphic passages than for the 20 percent ones.

MARTIN, CLESSEN J., & SHEFFIELD, CAROL. The effect of telegraphic prose on the reading behavior of blind and sighted students. *Journal of Applied Psychology,* August 1976, *61,* 513-518.
Examines the effects of telegraphic deletions upon the comprehension and reading rates of Braille and regular print readers. In Phase 1, 24 blind Braille readers from the Texas State School for the Blind (secondary school) and 164 sighted students from public secondary schools rank-ordered the words within each sentence of a 947-word passage according to relative importance in communicating the meaning of the sentence. Based on these rank-orderings, the less important words were deleted to construct for each sentence 10 percent, 30 percent, and 50 percent telegraphic deletions. In Phase 2, 144 sighted and 27 blind subjects read the full and telegraphic passages, and the authors recorded reading time, reading rate, and percent correct on 2 multiple-choice tests. A Kendall coefficient of concordance revealed significant agreement by the blind and sighted judges in Phase 1. In Phase 2, 30 percent and 50 percent deletions had a less deleterious effect on the reading performance of the Braille readers. While reading rates and comprehension scores decreased for the sighted readers as deletion level increased, scores for blind Braille readers were not adversely affected by the telegraphic passages.

MILLAR, SUSANNA. Effects of tactual and phonological similarity on the recall of Braille letters by blind children. *British Journal of Psychology,* May 1975, *66,* 193-201.
Probes tactual recall by 48 blind children, ages 5-9 to 8-0 on serial lists containing one to 6 Braille letters, which varied in confusability of feel and name sound.

MOMMERS, M.J.C. Braille reading: factors affecting achievement of Dutch elementary school children. *The New Outlook for the Blind,* October 1976, *70,* 332-340.
Compares reading skills of 120 Dutch visually-impaired children, ages 6 to 15, with those of sighted children between 1970 and 1973. In addition, the relationship between reading achievement and residual vision, hand movement during reading, verbal intelligence and haptic

perception was investigated. The blind subjects took 2 and 1-half times as long as sighted children to read separated unrelated words, though poor Braille readers tended to lag farther behind poor sighted readers than good Braille readers lagged behind good sighted readers. Amount of residual vision bore little relationship to reading ability, but the way a child moved his or her hand during reading bore a strong relationship. Verbal IQ, as measured on the verbal section of the WISC, showed a stronger relationship with reading achievement than did haptic perception. Of the various haptic measures used, form discrimination and figure orientation were more important than size and roughness discrimination.

MORRIS, JUNE E. Adaptation of the Durrell Listening-Reading Series for use with the visually handicapped. *Education of the Visually Handicapped,* Spring 1976, *8,* 21-27.
Tests the validity of a Braille and a large type edition of a reading-listening test. Subjects were 141 legally blind children able to read primer or higher level textbooks.

NEWMAN, J.D., & LAX, BERNARD. Evaluation of closed circuit TV reading systems for the partially sighted. *Journal of the American Optometric Association,* December 1972, *43,* 1362-1366.
Assesses use of closed circuit TV reading systems with 85 low-vision patients.

NOLAN, C.Y., & ASHCROFT, S.C. The visually handicapped. *Review of Educational Research,* 1969, *39,* 52-70.
Includes a review of research done in tactile reading between 1966 and 1968 in a general review of studies related to the visually handicapped.

NOLAN, CARSON Y. Blind children: degree of vision, mode of reading—a 1963 replication. *Optometric Weekly,* September 8, 1966, *57,* 29-34.
Compares data on enrollments of blind children as of January 1960, with those of January 1963, with regard to level of vision, mode of reading, and grade distributions.

OLSEN, MYRNA R.; HARLOW, STEVEN D.; WILLIAMS, JOHN D. An evaluation of McBride's approach to rapid reading for Braille and large print readers. *Education of the Visually Handicapped,* Spring 1977, *9,* 16-23.
Measures changes in reading rate and comprehension for 3 groups of visually handicapped readers, ages 10 to 65, after exposure to 16 hours of training in rapid reading techniques. Two groups of Braille readers (N=15; N=12) and one group of large print readers (N=10) were trained by different researchers using similar methods in 2 geographically distinct areas. Despite significant differences among the groups in

years of education, outside practice time and motivation for participating in the training, all 3 groups made significant gains in reading rate as measured by both formal and informal tests. Comprehension did not change significantly for any of the 3 groups after training.

REX, EVELYN J. A study of basal readers and experimental supplementary instructional materials for teaching primary reading in Braille. Part I: An analysis of Braille features in basal readers. *Education of the Visually Handicapped,* December 1970, *2,* 97-107.

Studies the use of contractions in vocabulary in four Braille basal readers, preprimer through third grade.

REX, EVELYN J. A study of basal readers and experimental supplementary instructional materials for teaching primary reading in Braille. Part II: Instructional materials for teaching reading in Braille. *Education of the Visually Handicapped,* March 1971, *3,* 1-7.

Studied 27 blind children reading at second- or third-grade level for eight weeks to test the effectiveness of supplementary instructional materials.

SLOAN, LOUISE L.; HABEL, ADELAIDE; & FEIOCK, KATHARINE. High illumination as an auxillary reading aid in diseases of the macula. *American Journal of Ophthalmology,* November 1973, *76,* 745-757.

Describes a simple clinical test to determine whether high illumination produces an improvement in the reading vision of patients with a macular lesion. Subjects ranged in age from 30 to 88 years old.

SYKES, KIM C. A comparison of the effectiveness of standard print and large print in facilitating the reading skills of visually impaired students. *Education of the Visually Handicapped,* December 1971, *3,* 97-105.

Analyzes whether standard print is less, equally, or more effective than large print for 41 visually impaired eighth- through twelfth-grade students ages 13 to 21.

THURMAN, DENNIS, & WEISS-KAPP, SHARON. Optacon instruction for the deaf-blind. *Education of the Visually Handicapped,* Summer 1977, *9,* 47-50.

Describes the process of instructing a 17-year-old deaf-blind student with the Optacon (an optical to tactile converter). The Optacon was viewed as a viable alternative for the input of print for this subject because of results of tests of verbal language and proprioceptive ability. Other criteria considered before selecting the subject for instruction included her motivation for learning the Optacon, the paucity of available current materials in Braille, and her inability to obtain information auditorily due to the severity of her hearing loss. After 35 to 40 months instruction, the subject had achieved 10-13 words per minute and 90-100 percent accuracy on selected test materials. Recommendations are offered to other users.

TUTTLE, DEAN W. A comparison of three reading media for the blind. *Education of the Visually Handicapped,* May 1972, *4,* 40-44.
Assesses comprehension of 104 Braille readers, ages 14-21, on three equivalent forms of a reading test: one in Braille, one in normal recording, and a third in compressed speech.

U.S. DEPARTMENT OF HEALTH, EDUCATION, AND WELFARE. *Blind children: degree of vision, mode of reading.* Washington, D.C.: U.S. Government Printing Offices, 1961.
Reports a survey of pupils in five states registered with the Office of Education by the American Printing House for the Blind made to determine visual acuity in relation to reading of print, Braille, or both.

WILLIS, DEBORAH HILL. Relationships between visual acuity, reading mode, and school systems for blind students. *Exceptional Children,* November 1979, *46,* 186-191.
Replicates earlier studies by the American Printing House for the Blind of the relationships among visual acuity, reading mode, grade level, and type of educational program for 26,433 blind students enrolled in educational programs receiving federal funds. The reading mode categories included Braille, Braille and large type, large type, large type and ink, regular ink, and aural. Overall, the distribution of students within nine categories of visual acuity or designation remained stable between this study and one conducted four years earlier. Since the earliest study in 1961, the proportion of students with more severe visual disorders gradually decreased, while the less severe categories increased. In general, the enrollment decreased. The number of regular ink and large type readers increased and the use of Braille decreased significantly. Aural reading material was used much more extensively.

WOOD, THOMAS A. The usability of the adapted Durrell Listening-Reading Series with students in the intermediate grades. *Education of the Visually Handicapped,* Summer 1979, *11,* 33-38.
Presents reliability and validity data related to the use of the *Durrell Listening-Reading Series* (DLRS) with 71 visually handicapped intermediate grade students. Subjects were selected from four residential schools for the blind and divided into two groups according

to their primary mode of reading: large print or Braille. Each group was administered the appropriate form of the Intermediate Level Listening and Reading Sections of the DLRS. Both Listening and Reading Tests, as well as the total DLRS, appeared to have a high degree of internal consistency. In addition, the correlation coefficients between the DLRS and the *Stanford Achievement Test* were significant, indicating criterion-related validity.

## Section 2. Visual Acuity and Efficiency

ANAPOLLE, LOUIS. Visual skills survey of dyslexic students. *Journal of American Optometric Association,* October 1967, *38,* 853-859.
Ascertains the effects of fusion amplitude, heterophoria, amblyopia, and other manifestations of stress on the visual performance of the reading task of 207 dyslexic students (178 males and 29 females) ages 8 to 18 years during three summers at a camp for remedial reading therapy.

ANGLE, JOHN, & WISSMANN, DAVID. A. Age, reading, and myopia. *American Journal of Optometry and Physiological Optics,* May 1978, *55,* 302-308.
Tests two theories of myopia, the use-abuse theory and the biological theory, to determine which explains the appearance and progression of myopia in a sample of 12- to 17-year-olds in the U.S. The use-abuse theory postulates that myopia is an outcome of continual focusing on a near object, as in reading. The biological theory predicts that either age from birth or age from puberty explains any tendency for myopia to appear. Data came from 6,295 individuals who had been included in Cycle III of the Health Examination Survey conducted jointly by the U.S. Public Health Service and the U.S. Bureau of the Census between March 1966 and March 1970. Regression analysis results indicated that education explained all the tendency of myopia to appear and progress among 12- to 17-year-olds. However, it was not shown that the amount of reading, as determined by highest level of education, was a major factor in explaining the whole distribution of myopia; rather, highest level of education accounted for only two percent of the variance of myopia.

ASHCROFT, SAMUEL C., & HARLEY, RENDALL K. The visually handicapped. *Review of Educational Research,* February 1966, *36,* 75-92.
Reviews 93 research studies in the area of the visually handicapped, published since 1963, and categorizes them under four main headings: general aspects, psychological aspects, education, and the multiply handicapped.

BEDWELL, C. H.; GRANT, R.; & MCKEOWN, J. R. Visual and ocular control anomalies in relation to reading difficulty. *British Journal of Educational Psychology,* February 1980, *50,* 61-70.

Describes an investigation into the relation among binocular function, ocular control, and reading difficulty in 25 poor readers and 15 good readers. Reading ability was assessed by the *Schonell R4 Test* and spelling ability was determined by the *Schonell Dictation Test E.* Poor readers had an average CA of 13-7 and average reading and spelling ages of 10-7 and 9-8, respectively. Good readers had an average CA of 13-7 and average reading and spelling ages of 13-6 and 13-8. Five tests of vision were administered: 1) a measure of static visual acuity using the Snellen, 2) a measure of binocular vision using the *Titmus Vision Screener,* 3) a measure of range of vision (the degree to which eyes can drift out of line and still see a single image) using polarized vectograms, 4) a measure of double vision using two slides that were slowly pulled apart and 5) a measure of dynamic viewing, or binocular eye behavior while reading aloud a passage from *Neale's Analysis of Reading Ability.* The data obtained from these static and dynamic tests were then compared for the successful and retarded reading groups. It was found that the retarded group showed a significant relation between anomalies of dynamic binocular viewing and reading attainment. On the tests under static viewing only one significant difference, poor stereopsis, could be found between the two groups.

BEDWELL, C. H.; GRANT, R.; & MCKEOWN, J. R. Visual and ocular control anomalies in relation to reading difficulty. *The British Journal of Educational Psychology,* November 1978, *48,* 355.

Presents an abstract of a study in which good and poor readers (based on the results of the *Neale Analysis*) were given visual acuity tests for distance vision on the Snellen Visual Acuity chart. Also measured was near- and far-point binocular acuity for static viewing and stereoscopic vision on a standard vision screener. The research supports, the authors concluded, that problems of dynamic viewing and ocular control while reading are important.

BING, LOIS B. Bibliography: visual problems in schools, 1945-1950. *Journal of the American Optometric Association,* May 1951, *22,* 596-605.

Classifies the references cited under the following major headings: causal factors in reading difficulty, eye-movement studies, perception, physical factors, reading rate, reading readiness, visual fatigue, and visual surveys in schools.

BING, LOIS B. A critical analysis of the literature on certain visual functions which seem to be related to reading achievement.

*Journal of the American Optometric Association,* March 1951, 22, 454-463.
Summarizes the essential findings of the relation of such visual functions as visual acuity, refractive errors, binocular coordination or muscle imbalance, fusion, and visual fields to reading achievement, and suggests possible explanations for wide differences in results.

BING, LOIS B. Vision readiness and reading readiness. In J. Allen Figurel (Ed.), *Improvement of reading through classroom practice,* International Reading Association Conference Proceedings, 1964, 9, 268-271.
Investigates the complex process of vision and its relationship to beginning reading, emphasizing the role of the teacher in recognizing symptoms of visual difficulty.

BROD, NATHAN, & HAMILTON, DAVID. Binocularity and reading. *Journal of Learning Disabilities,* November 1973, 6, 574-576.
Induces disturbances in binocular vision of 162 fifth graders classified as good, average, and poor readers in order to determine the effect of these disturbances on reading achievement.

CHERNICK, BRUCE. Profile of peripheral visual anomalies in the disabled reader. *Journal of the American Optometric Association,* October 1978, 49, 1117-1118.
Performs a visual screening on 80 disabled readers aged eight to eleven. Subjects scored two or more years below grade level in reading on the *Stanford Achievement Tests.* The sample included 49 males and 31 females. The results indicated a significantly higher percentage of failures in tests of fusion, accommodation, and oculomotor skills relative to visual acuity and ocular pathology. The author cites the need to include a more comprehensive vision screening to detect the visual problems most common in disabled readers.

CLELAND, DONALD L. Seeing and reading. *American Journal of Optometry and Archives of American Academy of Optometry,* September 1953, 30, 467-481.
Summarizes the results of more than 30 studies relating to types of cues to word recognition, nature of the reading process, visual factors in reading, and effect of prolonged reading on visual fatigue.

DEADY, MARION C. Visual factors in reading disability. *The Columbia Optometrist,* December 1952, 26, 5-7.
Discusses the nature of visual difficulties that are related to reading retardation, as reported in 11 previous investigations; suggests means of correcting and eliminating each defect.

DEMILLA, LORRAINE A. Visual fatigue and reading. *Journal of Education,* December 1968, *151,* 4-34.
Reviews 42 sources in discussing visual fatigue and reading, with special emphasis on the psychology of word perception, the determinants of legibility, and the role of various typographical factors.

EAMES, THOMAS H. Accommodation in school children: age five, six, seven, and eight years. *American Journal of Ophthalmology,* June 1961, *51,* 1255-1257.
Presents data on the near-point accommodative ability of 899 urban and suburban children to determine their visual readiness for school tasks.

EAMES, THOMAS H. Correlation between birth weight and visual acuity: from the age of five through twelve years. *American Journal of Ophthalmology,* December 1954, *38,* 850-851.
Compares the coefficients of correlation between birth weight and visual acuity in the case of 40 reading failures and 40 nonreading failures.

EAMES, THOMAS H. The effect of anisometropia on reading achievement. *American Journal of Optometry and Archives of American Academy of Optometry,* December 1964, *41,* 700-702.
Compares the reading performances of 25 children (median Chronological Age (CA) 9.8 years) having equal refractive anomalies in each eye and 25 children (median CA 9.6) having anisometropia to determine the effect of anisometropia on reading achievement and the improvement of reading resulting from correction of refractive defects, followed by regular classroom instruction.

EAMES, THOMAS H. The influence of hypermetropia and myopia on reading achievement. *American Journal of Ophthalmology,* March 1955, *39,* 375-377.
Compares the differences between the chronological age and reading age of 64 reading failures and 57 reading nonfailures, from the third and fourth grades, grouped according to refractive condition.

EAMES, THOMAS H. The relationship of birth weight, the speeds of object and word perception, and visual acuity. *Journal of Pediatrics,* November 1955, *47,* 603-606.
Compares the speed of object and word perception and visual acuity of 25 pupils whose birth weights were less than 5.5 pounds with those of an equal number whose birth weights were 5.5 pounds or over.

EAMES, THOMAS H. Visual handicaps to reading. *Journal of Education,* February 1959, *141,* 3-35.

Summarizes the comparative eye condition of reading failures and unselected groups of school children examined by the author over a long period of years.

EDSON, WILLIAM H.; BOND, GUY L.; & COOK, WALTER W. Relationships between visual characteristics and specific silent reading abilities. *Journal of Educational Research*, February 1953, *46*, 451-457.
Reports the results of a study to determine the relationship, if any, between variations in 10 measures of silent reading skills and 13 tests of visual characteristics in the case of 188 fourth-grade pupils in four schools of St. Paul, Minnesota.

EFRON, MARVIN. The role of vision in reading readiness. In J. Allen Figurel (Ed.), *Reading and Inquiry*, International Reading Association Conference Proceedings 1965, *10*, 357-358.
Discusses generally the role of visual skills in reading development.

FLAX, N. Problems in relating visual function to reading disorder. *American Journal of Optometry and Archives of the American Academy*, 1970, *47*, 366-371.
Presents an analysis of the relationship of visual function to reading.

GROSVENOR, THEODORE. Are visual anomalies related to reading ability? *Journal of the American Optometric Association*, April 1977, *48*, 510-517.
Discusses results of studies which provide information indicating a relationship between visual anomalies and reading disability. Reviews studies of astigmatism, strabismus, color vision anomolies, and myopia and hypermetropia.

GRUBER, ELLIS. Reading ability, binocular coordination and the ophthalmograph. *Archives of Ophthalmology*, March 1962, *67*, 280-288.
Makes an analysis of ophthalmographic records of 50 patients, ages 10 to 68 years, to determine the validity of the evidences of binocular coordination based on the findings of an ophthalmologist's examination.

HOLMES, JACK A. Visual hazards in the early teaching of reading. In Helen K. Smith (Ed.), *Perception and Reading*, Proceedings of the International Reading Association, 1968, 12(4), 53-61.
Cites 44 references in discussing the effects of early reading on vision.

HUELSMAN, CHARLES B. Some recent research on visual problems in reading. *American Journal of Optometry and Archives of American Academy of Optometry*, November 1958, *35*, 559-564.

Summarizes pertinent research since 1960 under three headings, outline form perception, use of the tachistoscope, and general visual achievement.

HULSMAN, HELEN L. Visual factors in reading: with implications for teaching. *American Journal of Ophthalmology,* November 1953, *36,* 1577-1580.
Discusses the effect of visual errors in reading and the results of correcting the defects of vision, as reported in a series of studies of these problems; also the implications of the findings and conclusions for the improvement of teaching.

HUNT, LYMAN C., JR., & SHELDON, WILLIAM D. Characteristics of the reading of a group of ninth grade pupils. *School Review,* September 1950, *58,* 348-353.
Presents an analysis of the scores of 19 good readers and 19 poor readers in the ninth grade on tests of reading, intelligence, personality, and vision.

JOSLIN, ETHEL S. Physical factors in reading. *The Columbia Optometrist,* December 1949, *23,* 6-7; February 1950, *24,* 5-6.
Presents a review of research on visual difficulties as causes of reading disability, with emphasis on visual acuity, refractive errors, myopia, astigmatism, binocular coordination, eye-muscle imbalance, fixation ability, and fusion.

KELLEY, DOROTHY JONES. Using children's school atypicalities to indicate ocular defects. *Journal of Educational Research,* February 1954, *47,* 455-462.
Correlates achievement scores in reading made by 533 pupils in grades 1 to 6 with Massachusetts Vision Test findings to determine the extent to which achievement scores and observation of visual behaviors or abnormalities could be used to indicate the presence of ocular defects.

KINGSTON, ALBERT J. (Ed.). Research for the classroom. Visual deficiencies and reading disability by Carl L. Rosen. *Journal of Reading,* October 1965, *9,* 57-61.
Presents a review of research, accompanied by a 40-item bibliography, of the role of visual deficiencies in causation of reading disability.

KNOX, GERTRUDE. Classroom symptons of visual efficiency. *Clinical Studies in Reading, 2,* 97-101. Supplementary educational monographs no. 77. Chicago: University of Chicago Press, 1953.
Presents evidence of the value of the classroom use of a checklist of 30 visual characteristics as determined through its application to 126 third-grade pupils, the results of a visual screening test being reported in the case of 41 pupils, and the findings of a refractionist in 37 cases.

KOETTING, JAMES F. Word recognition as a function of locus in the four lateral visual fields: the Iota Phenomenon. *American Journal of Optometry and Archives of American Academy of Optometry,* January 1970, *47,* 56-66.

Investigates the relative performance in each of four lateral peripheral visual fields using three-letter English words (from Dolch Basic Sight Vocabulary) with 46 fifth-grade subjects, and found a superiority of performance in the right binocular field as compared to the left, and in the total field of the left eye as compared to the right.

LAWSON, LAWRENCE J., JR. Ophthalmological factors in learning disabilities. In H. R. Myklebust (Ed.), *Progress in learning disabilities,* Vol. 1. New York: Grune & Stratton, 1968, 147-181.

Studies a group of 82 children with learning disabilities but of average or above mental ability to determine the nature of relationships between ocular conditions and learning disabilities.

LÉTOURNEAU, JACQUES E.; LAPIERRE, NICOLE; & LAMONT, ANNE. The relationship between convergence insufficiency and school achievement. *American Journal of Optometry and Physiological Optics,* January 1979, *56,* 18-22.

Screens 735 third- through sixth-grade children for convergence ability and determines whether convergence insufficiency is related to lower academic achievement. Each child was tested six times by one of two clinicians. The mean of the six readings was used. The 41 boys and 29 girls identified with abnormal convergence were then given a complete visual examination. A comparison was then made on academic achievement between 25 pupils who exhibited convergence insufficiency and 251 who did not. No significant differences were noted between groups in reading, spelling, composition, or grade point average.

NORN, M.S.; RINDZIUNSKI, EVA; & SKYDSGAARD, H. Ophthalmologic and orthoptic examinations of dyslextics. *Skolepsykologi,* 1970, 7, 333-349.

Compares the visual defects found by ophthalmologists among 117 dyslextics and a normal group matched for age, sex, class, and IQ.

PARK, GEORGE E. Ophthalmological aspects of learning disabilities. *Journal of Learning Disabilities,* April 1969, *2,* 189-198.

Synthesizes the visual process with the concept of homeostasis as applied to other physiological functions and balances and relates their influence in reading and draws eight conclusions from a review of research studies related to functional vision, visual acuity, and mirror and reversed vision in normal and dyslexic children.

PRINCE, JACK H. Relationship of reading types to uncorrectable lowered visual acuity. *American Journal of Optometry and*

*Archives of American Academy of Optometry*, November 1957, *34*, 581-595.

Presents experimental evidence secured to test the hypothesis "that with scientifically planned interletter spacing, print that is ordinarily visible only to subjects with emmetropia, can be made legible to subjects with a certain degree of uncorrected low visual acuity."

RICHARDS, OSCAR W. A comparison of acuity test letters with and without serifs. *American Journal of Optometry and Archives of American Academy of Optometry*, October 1965, *42*, 589-592.

Compares visual acuity on the Snellen Chart for 103 persons, ages 17 to 82, when two different types of letters were shown at two luminance levels.

ROBINSON, HELEN M. (Ed.). *Clinical Studies in Reading, II*. Supplementary Educational Monographs, No. 77. Chicago: University of Chicago Press, 1953.

Reports a series of studies of reading, with emphasis on visual problems, made by the staff members and graduate students doing work in the University of Chicago Reading Clinic.

ROBINSON, HELEN M. Diagnosis and treatment of poor readers with vision problems. *Clinical Studies in Reading, II*, 9-28. Supplementary Educational Monographs, No. 77. Chicago: The University of Chicago Press, 1953.

Presents illustrative case studies of poor readers with visual problems, describes methods of visual screening, and discusses problems involved in remedial therapy.

ROBINSON, HELEN M. Factors related to monocular and binocular reading efficiency. *American Journal of Optometry and Archives of American Academy of Optometry*, July 1951, *28*, 337-346.

Analyzes data secured from 75 cases to determine if middle-grade pupils read better monocularly or binocularly and if performance on the Gray Check Tests is related to scores on visual efficiency tests.

ROBINSON, HELEN M. Visual efficiency and reading status in the elementary school. In Helen M. Robinson & Helen K. Smith (Eds.), *Clinical Studies in Reading III*, Supplementary Educational Monographs No. 97. Chicago: The University of Chicago Press, 1968, 49-65.

Calculates coefficients of correlation and factor analyses to determine patterns of visual test scores related to reading achievement at each of the first eight grades and compares performance on each subtest of 10 visual screening batteries for 63 good and 60 poor readers.

ROBINSON, HELEN M., & HUELSMAN, CHARLES B., JR. Visual efficiency and progress in learning to read. *Clinical Studies in Reading, II,* 31-63. Supplementary Educational Monographs No. 77. Chicago: University of Chicago Press, 1953.

Reports the results of studies, including more than 50 pupils in grades 1, 4, and 8, to determine the relationship between visual efficiency and reading progress and to evaluate existing visual screening tests, determining their reliability and validity when used with elementary-school pupils varying in age and achievement.

ROBINSON, HELEN M., et al. An evaluation of the children's visual achievement forms at grade 1. *American Journal of Optometry and Archives of American Academy of Optometry,* October 1958, *35,* 1-11.

Reports correlations between scores made by 87 first-grade children on a battery of tests to evaluate the children's visual achievement forms as a predictor of reading achievement, skill in handwriting, and the need for visual examination.

ROSEN, CARL L. The status of school vision screening: A review of research and consideration of some selected problems. In G. B. Schick and M. M. May (Eds.) *The Psychology of Reading Behavior,* Yearbook of the National Reading Conference, 1969, *18,* 42-48.

Lists and evaluates current visual screening devices and batteries available for school purposes, as well as considering the accuracy of referral of several of the standard screening tests and pertinent factors which can influence this accuracy.

ROSENBLOOM, ALFRED A., JR. The relationship between aniseikonia and achievement in reading. In Helen M. Robinson & Helen K. Smith (Eds.), *Clinical Studies in Reading III,* Supplementary Educational Monographs No. 97. Chicago: The University of Chicago Press, 1968, 109-116.

Compares the incidence of aniseikonia and suppression exhibited by 40 retarded readers in grades 4 to 8 with a control group of equivalent size, age, and intelligence.

ROSENBLOOM, ALFRED A., JR. Promoting visual readiness for reading. In J. Allen Figurel (Ed.), *Changing Concepts of Reading Instruction,* International Reading Association Conference Proceedings, 6, 1961, 89-93.

Discusses the importance of visual readiness and its role in visual perception and the development and correction of visual problems, and stresses the need for a complete visual examination to be given before a child enters school.

SASSOON, HUMPHREY F.; DAVIS, MORTON; & O'CONNELL, ELLEN MARIE.
Vision tests as predictors of learning disabilities. *Journal of the American Optometric Association*, January 1977, *48*, 49-55.
Explores 3 screening tests for visual problems and studies the relationship to school achievement. The *Farnsworth Panel D-15 Test*, a color-matching test; the LRD test, a visual language field development test; and a test assessing speed of visual scan were administered to classes of children from 3 regular and 2 private schools for learning disabled. Subjects were rated on a 5-point scale based on their performance on a readiness or achievement test. The visual problems identified by these instruments were found to be related to poor school achievement. The authors suggest these tests for early detection of potential learning problems.

SCHUBERT, D. G. Induced refractive errors in human subjects. In F. A. Young & D. B. Lindsley (Eds.), *Early experience and visual information processing in perceptual and reading disorders*. Washington, D.C.: National Academy of Sciences, 1970, 62-68.
Presents 15 citations and emphasizes findings from two studies in a discussion of the effects of inducing myopia on far point tachistoscopic perception and of the effects of inducing astigmatism on various visual, psychological, and physical problems.

SCHUBERT, DELWYN G., & WALTON, HOWARD N. Effects of induced astigmatism. *The Reading Teacher*, March 1968, *21*, 547-551.
Analyzes the difficulties which 35 seniors (ages 22 to 47) from a college of optometry encountered when taking a test while subjected to 1.00 diopter of induced astigmatism with-the-rule.

SCHUSTER, D. H.; KARAS, G. G.; & ANTONELLI, D. C. Some normative data on reading distance. *Perceptual and Motor Skills*, 1969, *28*, 202.
Presents data concerning reading distance for high school graduates.

SHEARRON, GILBERT F. Color deficiency and reading achievement in primary school boys. *The Reading Teacher*, March 1969, *22*, 510-512, 577.
Screens 1,295 grade 1, 2, and 3 pupils for color deficiency and investigates the difference between the reading achievement of 35 color-deficient boys and 35 non-color-deficient boys.

SHULMAN, PAUL F. The vision specialist in a remedial reading program. *Optometric Weekly*, December 13, 1951, *43*, 1941-1945.
Reviews the results of 20 studies relating to causation of reading disability to determine if vision tests alone can diagnose reading deficiency and if there is a definite syndrome of visual factors associated with reading difficulty.

SILBIGER, FRANCENE. Visual test score differences between high and low reading achievement groups among college freshmen. In D. M. Wark (Ed.), *College and Adult Reading,* Yearbook of the North Central Reading Association, *5,* 1968, 134-145.
Inquires whether visual skills measured by the Titmus Optical Vision Tester were related to reading achievement with 38 students who scored low on a speed of comprehension test and 25 who scored high who were then each given 12 visual screening tests.

SILBIGER, FRANCENE, & WOOLF, DANIEL. Perceptual difficulties associated with reading disability. In C. A. Ketcham (Ed.), *Proceedings of the College Reading Association,* 1965, *6,* 98-102.
Relates reading ability and academic achievement to visual discomfort and visual disability for 90 undergraduates—37 were in a poor achievement group and 53 were in a good group.

SMITH, HELEN K. Identification of factors that inhibit progress in reading. In J. Allen Figurel (Ed.), *Reading and Inquiry,* International Reading Association Conference Proceedings, 1965, *10,* 200-202.
Discusses methods of identifying specific factors related to reading retardation.

SMITH, KARL U.; SCHREMSER, ROBERT; & PUTZ, VERNON. Binocular coordination in reading. *Journal of Applied Psychology,* June 1971, *55,* 251-258.
Uses real-time laboratory computer methods to determine the differences between the two eyes in reading for three subjects, each having 18 trials.

SMITH, WILLIAM. Report of vision screening tests in a group of ten reading problem cases. *American Journal of Optometry and Archives of American Academy of Optometry,* June 1955, *32,* 295-303.
Presents 10 case studies in which both eye examination under cycloplegia and stereoscopic instrument tests were used to test the assumption that discrepancies exist between the results of the two types of examinations.

SOLAN, HAROLD A. Learning disabilities: the role of the developmental optometrist. *Journal of the American Optometric Association,* November 1979, *50,* 1259-1266.
Describes the role of the optometrist in treating children with learning disabilities. The author states that anyone experiencing learning disorders should see an optometrist periodically. The literature does not support the conclusion that a high correlation exists between visual acuity and learning to read. Visual disorders and their

relationship to reading problems are briefly described along with citations to the research literature in these areas. Etiological, diagnostic, and therapeutic factors in learning disorders are discussed, stressing visual functional disorders, perceptual-motor and developmental lags, and cognitive style. Research in these various areas is briefly referred to.

SPACHE, GEORGE D. Classroom reading and the visually handicapped child. In J. Allen Figurel (Ed.), *Changing concepts of reading instruction,* International Reading Association Conference Proceedings, 1961, *6,* 93-97.
Explores changes that have occurred in thinking about reading and the visually handicapped child and examines the problems of etiology and symptoms in adequate diagnosis.

SPACHE, GEORGE D., & TILLMAN, CHESTER E. A comparison of the visual profiles of retarded and nonretarded readers. *Journal of Developmental Reading,* Winter 1962, *5,* 101-109.
Presents a comparison of performance on a visual screening battery by 114 retarded readers with 101 nonretarded readers selected from files of a reading clinic.

STARNES, DAVID R. Visual abilities vs. reading abilities. *Journal of the American Optometric Association,* June 1969, *40,* 596-600.
Describes a pilot study of the relationship between visual abilities or visual perception and the ability to learn to read among 18 third-grade students who were divided into 8 good readers and 10 poor readers and tested with a group of visual abilities tests and several visual-perceptual-motor tests.

STEINBAUM, MILTON, & KURK, MITCHELL. Comparison of visual performance in two classes of below average readers. *Journal of the American Optometric Association,* October 1956, *35,* 194-196.
Compares the visual status of two groups of below average readers, namely, 17 fourth-grade pupils with greater average retardation in reading and 18 fifth-grade pupils with lesser average retardation.

STEINBAUM, MILTON, & KURK, MITCHELL. Relationship between the Keystone Visual Skills Test with reading achievement and intelligence. *American Journal of Optometry,* April 1958, *35,* 173-181.
Compares the visual scores made by 100 fifth- and sixth-grade pupils, classified into three IQ groups and into "above" and "below average" in reading, to determine the relationship between the scores on the Keystone Visual Skills Test and reading, intelligence, and reading and intelligence combined.

STEINBERG, PHILIP M., & ROSENBERG, ROBERT. Relationship between reading and various aspects of visual anomalies. *Journal of the American Optometric Association,* March 1956, *26,* 444-446.
Summarizes relationships, based on data from 1,000 children in grades 4 to 8 inclusive, between reading ability and ocular muscle imbalances, vertical muscle imbalances, hand dominance, hand-eye dominance, and visual acuity and depth perception.

TOWNSEND, AGATHA. What research says to the reading teacher: A bibliography on sensory handicaps. *The Reading Teacher,* May 1966, *19,* 677-681.
Presents an annotated bibliography of 18 reports dealing with reading research related to pupils with visual, auditory, and speech impairment.

TRACHTMAN, JOSEPH N. The visual environment of the classroom and learning. *Optometric Weekly,* February 3, 1972, *63,* 106-110.
Summarizes research dealing with vision and illumination with special emphasis on classroom lighting.

WALTON, HOWARD N., & SCHUBERT, DELWYN N. Induced myopia and far point perception. *American Journal of Optometry and Archives of American Academy of Optometry,* May 1965, *42,* 311-314.
Reports a study in which the Keystone Standard Tachistoscope was used to determine what effects varying degrees of artificially induced myopia have on far point perception of 24 college seniors ranging from 21 to 38 years old and who manifested 20/20 visual acuity.

WILSON, W. KEITH, & WOLD, ROBERT W. School vision screening implications for optometry. *Optometric Weekly,* May 1970, *61,* 488-493.
Reports the results of visual symptoms and visual screening of 79 middle-grade pupils in the upper quartile in reading compared to 81 middle-grade pupils in the lower quartile (by way of the Stanford Reading Test).

YOUNG, F. A.; LEARY, G. A.; BALDWIN, W. R.; WEST, D. C.; BOX, R. A.; GOO, F. J.; HARRIS, E.; & JOHNSON, C. Refractive errors, reading performance and school achievement among Eskimo children. *American Journal of Optometry and Archives of the American Academy of Optometry,* 1970, *47,* 384-390.
Explores the relationship between vertical refractive errors and various measures of reading and school achievement for 204 Eskimo children. Data for Eskimo and Caucasian children are compared.

YOUNG, FRANCIS A. Reading measures of intelligence and refractive errors. *American Journal of Optometry and Archives of*

*American Academy of Optometry,* May 1963, *40,* 257-264. Determines relationships, based on tests given to 117 pupils (ages not given), between hyperopia or myopia and intelligence (measured by the Stanford-Binet and the California Test of Mental Maturity), and obtains a partial correlation with reading held constant by use of the Durrell-Sullivan Reading Achievement Test scores.

# Part 2
# Visual Perception

**The section of this bibliography on visual perception** incorporates such diverse topics as visual memory, visual modality, and visual discrimination.

AARON, I. E. Translating research into practice: reading readiness, visual perception, auditory perception. In Helen K. Smith (Ed.), *Perception and Reading,* International Reading Association Conference Proceedings, 12, Part 4, 1968, 130-135.
Discusses the changes in teacher practices caused by research findings and the hazards of interpreting reading research results, and summarizes the strengths, limitations, and implications for practice of six research studies.

ALIOTTI, NICHOLAS C. Tendency to mirror-image on a visual memory test. *Academic Therapy,* January 1980, *15,* 261-267.
Tests aspects of the reversal phenomenon by administering a test of immediate visual memory requiring children to select among six alternatives a previously exposed geometric design. Among the alternatives were a mirror-image and a rotation. The Bannatyne Visual-Spatial Memory test was administered to 37 children in private preschools, 116 children in K-2, 19 cerebral palsied children (CA of 5-6 to 15-1), and 16 children in a learning disabilities class (CA of 7-9 to 12-10). There was some tendency for mirror-image reversal choice to represent a fairly common error. For the total sample the percentage of correct matches and error choices were: original match, 45 percent; mirror-image reversal, 14 percent; fragmentation, 13 percent; complication, 11 percent; rotation, 8 percent; and simplification, 8 percent.

ALLINGTON, RICHARD L. Developmental trends in the discrimination of high frequency words. In P. David Pearson (Ed.), Reading: theory, research, and practice. *Twenty-Sixth Yearbook of the National Reading Conference,* 1977, 187-192.

Examines the developmental nature of visual discrimination abilities for 275 children from grades K-3. A total of 120 words from 3 widely used basic word lists were used as stimuli. Target words were embedded among 4 distractors, each of which had some letters in common with it. A large gain occurred in scores between kindergarten and grade 1, a lesser improvement between grades 1 and 2, and a leveling effect with virtually no gain between grades 2 and 3. Additional analysis showed a lack of effect for school type (urban, rural, suburban) and for sex in grades 1, 2, and 3.

ALLINGTON, RICHARD. Cue selection and discrimination learning. *Academic Therapy,* Spring 1975, *10,* 339-343.
Discusses implications of several studies of letter discrimination for beginning reading, focusing on use of color cues. The study involved 102 kindergarteners.

ALLINGTON, RICHARD L.; GORMLEY, KATHLEEN; & TRUEX, SHARON. Poor and normal readers' achievement on visual tasks involving high frequency, low discriminability words. *Journal of Learning Disabilities,* May 1976, *9,* 292-296.
Tests the perceptual deficit hypothesis using tasks of matching, recognition, reproduction from memory, and oral reading of isolated words. Subjects were 12 below average and 12 above average third grade readers in a suburban school.

AMORIELL, WILLIAM J. Reading achievement and the ability to manipulate visual and auditory stimuli. *Journal of Learning Disabilities,* October 1979, *12,* 562-563.
Seeks to provide information on the relationship between reading achievement and the ability to manipulate sequential stimuli within and between auditory and visual modalities. Fifty-two retarded readers and 53 average and above average readers were included in the study. Third graders identified as retarded readers met these criteria: 1) no visual acuity or discrimination deficits, 2) no auditory acuity or discrimination deficits, 3) average in intelligence (WISC, Stanford-Binet, or Slosson Intelligence Test), and 4) retarded in reading achievement. For the average and above average third-grade readers, the first three criteria were identical and they performed average or above in reading on an informal reading inventory. The perceptual tests, administered to all except five absentees, included two tests to assess the ability to manipulate sequential stimuli within the visual and auditory fields and two additional tests to assess the ability to integrate sequential stimuli between the visual and auditory modalities. A significant difference favoring the better readers was found on the test of visual sequential memory for letters.

ARNETT, JOHN L., & DILOLLO, VINCENT. Visual information processing in relation to age and to reading ability. *Journal of
Experimental Child Psychology,* February 1979, *27,* 143-152.
Developmentally compares temporal integration and backward
masking task responses of forty-eight good and poor male readers,
ages 7, 9, 11, and 13. Poor readers were identified as those whose scores
fell below grade placement on the *Stanford Achievement Test.* Good
readers were identified as those with above grade level reading
performance on the SAT. Results revealed no difference between
groups in visual persistence or processing rate, but processing rate
increased with chronological age of both levels of readers.

ASHLOCK, PATRICK. The visual perception of children in the primary
grades and its relation to reading performance. In J. A. Figurel
(Ed.), *Reading and Inquiry,* Proceedings of the International
Reading Association, 10, 1965, 331-333.
Reports correlations between scores of 90 first-, second-, and
third-grade children on a battery of tests measuring reading
performance and three types of visual perception to determine the
relationship between reading and types of visual perception, and the
importance of visual perception as a predictor of reading achievement.

BADIAN, NATHLIE A. Auditory-visual integration, auditory memory,
and reading in retarded and adequate readers. *Journal of
Learning Disabilities,* February 1977, *10,* 108-114.
Undertakes a study to determine the nature of the inferior performance
of retarded readers in auditory-visual integration tasks. Subjects were
30 retarded and 30 adequate readers, 10 each from grades 3, 4, and 5.
Determination of reading retardation was based on a formula for
learning disability that included reading age *(Gray Oral Reading Test*
and the *Reading Comprehension* subtest of the *Stanford Diagnostic
Reading Test)* and expectancy age. Subjects were given visual,
auditory, and memory tasks underlying auditory-visual integration
along with 7 auditory-visual integration tests placing varying
demands upon short-term auditory memory. The 2 groups differed
significantly on all tasks. The performance of retarded readers
deteriorated sharply as memory demands increased, a finding not
found for adequate readers. The author concludes that a short-term
memory deficit seems to be a factor in the poorer auditory-visual
integration performance of retarded readers.

BAKKER, D. J. Sensory dominance and reading ability. *Journal of
Communication Disorders,* n.m. 1967, *1,* 316-318.
Relates the reading achievement scores to competency in estimating
the midpoint of a bar using the visual and the tactile-kinaesthetic
modality for 100 7- to 11-year-old Dutch boys and girls, matched on age.

BALMUTH, MIRIAM. Visual and auditory modalities: how important are they? In Nila B. Smith (Ed.), *Current Issues in Reading,* International Reading Association Conference Proceedings, *13,* 1969, 165-177.

Reviews research in visual and auditory modalities by investigating (1) the superiority of one modality over another, (2) the simultaneous use of different modalities, and (3) modality studies focused on reading.

BANNATYNE, A. Psychological bases of reading in the United Kingdom. In Marion D. Jenkinson (Ed.), *Reading Instruction: An International Forum,* Proceedings of the International Reading Association World Congress on Reading, 1, 1967, 327-335.

Cites 15 sources in discussing verbal and visuo-spatial ability differences in boys and girls.

BARRETT, THOMAS. Visual discrimination and reading: an educator's viewpoint. *The Optometric Weekly,* October 1969, *60,* 36-41.

Analyzes the results of three discrimination studies and their relationship to success in beginning reading, with an emphasis on visual discrimination in the first study, visual and auditory discrimination in the second, and visual perception skills from the Frostig program in the third.

BARRETT, THOMAS C. Performance on selected prereading tasks and first grade reading achievement. In J. Allen Figurel (Ed.), *Vistas in Reading,* International Reading Association Conference Proceedings, 11(1), 1966, 461-464.

Outlines a study showing predictive relationships between certain prereading tasks and reading achievement.

BARRETT, THOMAS C. Visual discrimination tasks as predictors of first grade reading achievement. *The Reading Teacher,* January 1965, *18,* 276-282.

Uses stratified random sampling techniques to select 632 first graders in ascertaining the relative contribution and total relationship of nine reading readiness variables (seven involving visual discrimination) to predict first-grade reading achievement.

BATEMAN, BARBARA. The efficacy of an auditory and a visual method of first grade reading instruction with auditory and visual learners. In Helen K. Smith (Ed.), *Perception and Reading,* Proceedings of the International Reading Association, 12(4), 1968, 105-112.

Involves four control and four experimental classrooms totaling 182 pupils in a study which explored the efficacy of an auditory approach compared with a visual approach to first-grade reading.

BEERY, JUDITH W. Matching of auditory and visual stimuli by average and retarded readers. *Optometric Weekly*, January 1970, *61*, 93-96.
Replicates the Birch-Belmont investigation with modifications, and compares a visual-auditory (V-A) presentation with auditory-visual (A-V) presentation using 15 retarded and 15 normal readers who ranged in age from 8 to 13 years and from 86 to 114 in IQ.

BEERY, JUDITH WILLIAMS. Matching of auditory and visual stimuli by average and retarded readers. *Child Development*, September 1967, *38*, 827-833.
Compares performance on three tasks of auditory-visual integration for 15 subjects (age range 8 years 9 months to 13 years 3 months) with specific reading disability and an equal number of controls.

BELL, ANNE E., & AFTANAS, M. S. Some correlates of reading retardation. *Perceptual and Motor Skills*, October 1972, *35*, 659-667.
Tests the efficacy of a battery of perceptual, visual-motor, and intellectual tests given to preschool children against their reading achievement at the end of first grade to describe the incipient retarded reader.

BELMONT, IRA; FLEGENHEIMER, HANNAH; & BIRCH, HERBERT G. Comparison of perceptual training and remedial instruction for poor beginning readers. *Journal of Learning Disabilities*, April 1973, *6*, 230-235.
Compares the effect of supplementary perceptual training and remedial instruction on the performance of 32 children identified as poor risks for beginning reading.

BENENSON, THEA FUCHS. Prediction of first-grade reading achievement: criterion validation of a measure of visual recognition memory. *Educational and Psychological Measurement*, Summer 1974, *34*, 423-427.
Uses stepwise multiple regression technique to assess effectiveness of short and long term visual memory for form, orientation, and sequence with readiness tests in predicting first grade reading achievement. Subjects were 105 boys and 87 girls in a white, upper middleclass suburban community.

BENGER, KATHLYN. The relationships of perception, personality, intelligence, and grade one reading achievement. In Helen K. Smith (Ed.), *Perception and Reading*, Proceedings of the International Reading Association, 12(4), 1968, 112-123.
Studies through linear multiple regression analysis the contribution of auditory discrimination, aural vocabulary, intelligence, teacher ratings of personality, and five aspects of visual perception in the

prediction of reading scores of 30 pairs of Canadian children at the end of first grade.

BIEGER, ELAINE. Effectiveness of visual training of letters and words on reading skills of nonreaders. *The Journal of Educational Research,* January/February 1978, *71,* 157-160.
Uses 43 second and third grade nonreaders who were diagnosed as having visual perceptual deficiencies and assigns the subjects randomly to experimental and control conditions. The experimental group received training in visual analysis, which included visual short-term memory, visual discrimination of letters and words, and remedial instruction. The control group received only remedial instruction. After 7 months, there were no significant differences between the groups in visual perception or achievement of reading skills. Experimental subjects gained 8.9 months in reading achievement, while the controls gained 9.2 months.

BILSKY, LINDA H.; EVANS, ROSS A.; & MARTIN, PAULA. Relative effectiveness of various letter discrimination procedures in directionality pretraining. *American Journal of Mental Deficiency,* January 1975, *79,* 359-366.
Investigates feedback, task format, problem type, and redundancy in teaching 56 institutionalized, mentally retarded adolescents and 52 educable, mentally retarded primary school children to discriminate confusable letters.

BIRCH, HERBERT G., & BELMONT, LILLIAN. Auditory-visual integration, intelligence and reading ability in school children. *Perceptual and Motor Skills,* February 1965, *20,* 295-305.
Reports the significance of developmental pattern of auditory-visual equivalence among a total of 220 children in kindergarten through grade 6 and correlates the pattern scores with intellectual status and reading achievement of pupils at each grade level.

BIRCH, HERBERT G., & BELMONT, LILLIAN. Auditory-visual integration in normal and retarded readers. *American Journal of Orthopsychiatry,* October 1964, *34,* 852-861.
Compares the performance of 150 retarded and 50 normal readers (all boys between the ages of 9.4 and 10.4 years with IQs higher than 80) on an auditory-visual pattern test developed by the authors to test the hypothesis that impairment in auditory-visual integration would occur more commonly in retarded than in normal readers.

BLACK, F. WILLIAM. Cognitive, academic, and behavioral findings in children with suspected and documented neurological dysfunction. *Journal of Learning Disabilities,* March 1976, *9,* 182-187.

Compares matched samples of 25 children with known brain damage and 25 children with suspected neurological dysfunction on tests of intelligence, visual perception, and academic achievement and on ratings by a neurologist and a psychologist.

BLACK, F. WILLIAM. Neurological dysfunction and reading disorders. *Journal of Learning Disabilities,* May 1973, *6,* 313-316.
Investigates intellectual ability, visual perception, and achievement of 2 samples of 25 children with reading disorders attributed to neurological disorders and compares performance based on hemispheric deficits.

BOOS, R. W. Dominance and control: relation to reading achievement. *Journal of Educational Research,* 1970, *63,* 466-470.
Reports findings on the relation of eye dominance and eye control to reading achievement from tests given to 273 eighth-grade students remaining from an earlier study which tested them at the second-grade level.

BOUMA, H., & LEGEIN, CH. P. Foveal and parafoveal recognition of letters and words by dyslexics and by average readers. *Neuropsychologia,* 1977, *15(1),* 69-80.
Investigates visual recognition of single letters and embedded letters with normal and dyslexic readers. More specifically, the recognition and storage of graphic information contained in both the foveal center and that contained just outside the foveal center (parafoveal or 1 degree visual angle) was examined. Twenty normal and 20 dyslexic readers, aged 9 to 14, participated in the study. Results indicated that both groups did equally well on isolated letters; however, the dyslexics generally stayed behind on embedded letters and on words. The authors discuss the results in terms of specific deficits on processes such as eye control, word recognition, and storage.

BOWER, THOMAS G. R. Reading by eye. In Harry Levin & Joanna P. Williams (Eds.), *Basic studies in reading.* New York: Basic Books, 1970, 134-146.
Details several experiments which used college students as subjects and attempted to obtain insight into the visual process nature of reading.

BRADLEY, BETTY HUNT. Differential responses in perceptual ability among mentally retarded brain-injured children. *Journal of Educational Research,* April 1964, *57,* 421-424.
Compares the performances of two groups of 35 mentally retarded brain-injured children on two tests of perceptual abilities with both groups paired in terms of chronological age, mental age, and IQ and originally differentiated on the basis of visual perceptual disabilities.

BRAUN, CARL. Interest-loading and modality effects on textual response acquisition. *Reading Research Quarterly,* Spring 1969, *4,* 428-444.
Investigates the differential rate of acquisition and retention of textual responses categorized on the basis of sex-related interest loading by presenting the texts to a sample of 240 kindergarten children in two modalities: auditory and auditory-visual.

BRIGGS, RAYMOND, & HOCEVAR, DENNIS J. A new distinctive feature theory for upper case letters. *The Journal of General Psychology,* July 1975, *93,* 87-93.
Validates a similarity index of printed capital letters based on distinctive feature analysis by predicting confusability on 7 previously published visual confusion matrices empirically generated in a variety of ways.

BRUININKS, R.H. Teaching word recognition to disadvantaged boys. *Journal of Learning Disabilities,* 1970, *3,* 28-37.
Assesses whether the use of teaching approaches consistent with the auditory or visual perceptual strengths of 40 economically-disadvantaged boys would facilitate their ability to learn and retain a list of unknown words.

BRUNER, JEROME S., & MINTURN, A. LEIGH. Perceptual identification and perceptual organization. *Journal of General Psychology,* July 1955, *53,* 21-28.
Reports the results of a study using 24 students as subjects to determine whether the operation of the closure principle in visual perception is affected by how the figure in which closure may occur is identified.

BRYAN, QHENTIN R. Relative importance of intelligence and visual perception in predicting reading achievement. *California Journal of Educational Research,* January 1964, *15,* 44-48.
Administers a battery of tests, including intelligence, readiness, visual perception, and reading achievement, to all children in kindergarten through grade 3 (N=21 to 25 per class) in a California school to determine the importance of the test scores in predicting reading comprehension and vocabulary.

BUDOFF, MILTON, & QUINLAN, DONALD. Auditory and visual learning in primary grade children. *Child Development,* June 1964, *35,* 583-586.
Tests the hypothesis that young children learn more rapidly by auditory than by visual stimulation by giving 56 pupils, ages 7 to 8 years, paired associates of familiar three- and four-letter nouns and verbs to determine the number of trials required to obtain the criterion when each modality was used.

BUDOFF, MILTON, & QUINLAN, DONALD. Reading progress as related to efficiency of visual and aural learning in the primary grades. *Journal of Educational Psychology,* October 1964, *55,* 247-252. Compares learning efficiency of 28 average and 28 retarded second-grade readers when meaningful words were presented aurally and visually in a paired-associate paradigm.

BUKTENICA, NORMAN A. Perceptual/social aspects of learning to read: a transactional process. *Peabody Journal of Education,* April 1977, *54,* 154-161. Describes the third-year findings of a project undertaken to lower the rate of social and academic difficulty among children and to prevent occurrence of later difficulty. All first-grade classes in a semi-rural Tennessee county were divided into 4 treatment groups: 1) supplementary perceptual instruction, 2) human development program, 3) both perceptual training and human development, and 4) no intervention. Teachers were assigned to workshops and in-service programs depending on their assignment group. At the beginning of grade 1, all pupils were administered one of 3 readiness tests, the Visual Motor Integration Test, the Test of Non-Verbal Auditory Discrimination and the Otis-Lennon Mental Abilities Test. At the end of grade 1, the Metropolitan Achievement Tests were given. Other instruments assessed teacher-pupil interaction and children's adaptation. Teacher expectations were of equal importance with either auditory or visual skills in predicting end of grade 1 reading scores. When visual and auditory scores were combined, the combination was a better predictor of grade 1 reading scores than was teacher expectation. Children who received supplemental perceptual training scored better on 3 of 5 reading subtests than did the control group.

BUSBY, W. A., & HURD, D. E. Relationships of auditory and visual reaction times to reading achievement. *Perceptual and Motor Skills,* 1968, *27,* 447-450. Investigates the relationship between reading achievement and the reaction time of an individual responding to auditory and visual stimuli present in his perceptual field. A random sample of forty pupils from each of grades two, four, and six with an equal proportion of boys and girls, provided the data for the study.

BUSWELL, G. T. The relationship between perceptual and intellectual processes in reading. *California Journal of Educational Research,* May 1957, *8,* 99-103. Reports the results of studies based on the hypothesis "that difficulties in reading for many college students are due to lack of perceptual skill" which results from "the fixing of perceptual habits in the elementary school before a sufficiently high level of maturity is reached."

BUTLER, DAVID C., & MILLER, LEON K. Role of order of approximation to English and letter array length in the development of visual laterality. *Developmental Psychology,* September 1979, *15,* 522-529.
Gives tachistoscopically presented arrays of English words and pseudo-words to seven- to ten-year-olds and notes hemifield superiority for recognition. A right hemifield superiority was found for all children and conditions. Five letter arrays produced a marked advantage for first letters in the right hemifield but this was not true for three letter arrays. The influence of orthographic structure appeared at all age levels and in both hemifields. The results are interpreted as suggesting that although a left to right postexposural scanning process may contribute to general hemifield asymmetries, their change with age is more likely associated with other factors.

CALDWELL, E. C., & HALL, V. C. The influence of concept training on letter discrimination. *Child Development,* 1969, *40,* 63-71.
Groups 72 kindergarten pupils randomly into one of three training groups to study the effect of training on letter discrimination ability.

CARMON, AMIRON; NACHSHON, ISRAEL; ISSEROFF, AMI; & KLEINER, MURRAY. Visual field differences in reaction times to Hebrew letters. *Psychonomic Science,* August 1972, *28,* 222-224.
Compares visual field superiority in reaction time to verbal stimuli which could be influenced by the direction of reading associated with the stimuli, using 6 or fewer students in each of 3 experiments.

CARROLL, JAMES L. A visual memory scale (VMS) designed to measure short-term recognition memory in five- and six-year-old children. *Psychology in the Schools,* April 1972, *9,* 152-158.
Develops a test of visual memory which requires recognition of visual forms rather than reproduction, and compares it with a battery of other instruments. Subjects were 198 kindergarten children and 32 educable retarded children, 13 of whom had central nervous system impairment.

CARROLL, JULIA A.; FULLER, GERALD B.; & CARROLL, JAMES L. Comparison of culturally deprived school achievers and underachievers on memory function and perception. *Perceptual and Motor Skills,* February 1979, *48,* 59-62.
Examines differences between culturally deprived achievers (N=18) and underachievers (N=18) on tests of visual-motor, spatial relationships, auditory recall, and visual memory. Scores on the Reading, Spelling, and Arithmetic sections of the Wide Range Achievement Test (WRAT) were used to determine underachievers (six months or more below expected grade level) and achievers (five months or less below expected level). In addition to the WRAT, subjects were given

the Peabody Picture Vocabulary Test, the Block Design subtest of the WISC, the Minnesota Percepto-Diagnostic Test, and the Memory-for-Designs Test. A significant difference was found between the two groups on the Minnesota Percepto Diagnostic Test only with achievers performing better than underachievers. The author hypothesizes that the differences are a function of the level of motor execution.

CARTER, DONALD E.; SPERO, A. JUNE; & WALSH, JAMES A. A comparison of the visual aural digit span and the Bender Gestalt as discriminators of low achievement in the primary grades. *Psychology in the Schools,* April 1978, *15,* 194-198.
Compares Koppitz's Visual Auditory Span Test (VADS) and the Bender Visual Motor Gestalt Test in their ability to discriminate low from average achievers in arithmetic skills (math concepts and math problem solving) and reading skills (reading vocabulary and reading comprehension) as measured by the Iowa Test of Basic Skills. A sample of 78 normal children, ages 6, 7, and 8, was administered the verbal portion of the WISC-R, VADS, the Bender and the Iowa. Covarying on Verbal IQ, the Bender-Gestalt discriminated low achievers (nine months below the expected grade equivalent) from average (all others) in vocabulary, math concepts, and problem solving; the VADS discriminated low from average achievers only for vocabulary and math concepts. Neither discriminated between low and average students on reading comprehension. Coefficients of correlation between age and IQ and the two perceptual tests are also reported.

CASSEL, RUSSELL N., & KLAS, JOHN O. Using factor analysis to compare test data. *California Journal of Educational Research,* May 1975, *26,* 137-144.
Utilizes factor analysis and multiple regression in attempting to determine which tests from a screening battery of IQ, perceptual, and readiness tests contribute least to the predictive ability of the total battery. Forty-five subjects aged 6 to 9 were administered the Frostig Visual Perception Test, the Stanford-Binet Intelligence Scale, the Metropolitan Achievement Test (Primary Battery), and tests of visual motor integration. In addition, scores of teacher ratings from 6 sub-scales on the Klas Teacher Rating Scales were utilized. A total of 21 variables were assessed. Reading competency, perceptual motor ability (figure ground), teacher ratings of social-emotional control, visual motor integration, arithmetic competency, verbal intelligence, and age were found to account for 75 percent of the total variance from all 21 variables.

CHANSKY, NORMAN M. Perceptual training with elementary school underachievers. *Journal of School Psychology,* January 1963, *1,* 33-41.

Compares reading and spelling scores after 10 weeks of 34 underachieving pupils, grades 3 and 4, who were placed in four groups: 12 who received remedial reading and perceptual training, eight who received just remedial reading, seven who received just perceptual training, and seven who received neither type of training.

CHIANG, CHUN. Gross vision of a word enhances the perceptibility of component letters: a model. *Vision Research*, 1978, *18*, 1599-1600.

Utilizes previous research findings in building a quantitative model to explain the order of accuracy for recognizing letters in meaningful words and non-related words. The model states that minimum features required for recognition of the whole pattern are equivalent to or less than the total features required for its component patterns. In addition, the features extracted in vision are related to the feature density and the field of attention.

CHURCH, MARILYN. Does visual perception training help beginning readers? *The Reading Teacher,* January 1974, *27,* 361-364.

Compares a formal with an informal visual perceptual training program, for 90 kindergarten children, on reading readiness and reading achievement.

CLIFTON-EVEREST, I. M.. Dyslexia: Is there a disorder of visual perception? *Neuropsychologia*, 1976, *14(4)*, 491-494.

Compares the visual processing strategies of dyslexics and nondyslexics. Using normal readers and dyslexics, aged 8 to 11, and a group of adults, subjects were asked to quickly determine if certain letter combinations were present or not present in stimulus words. Results indicated that some dyslexics fail to acquire skills of visual analysis that exploit the sequential structure of written words, as evidenced in their speed of identifying letter sequences in words.

CLIFTON-EVEREST, I. M. The immediate recognition of tachistoscopically presented visual patterns by backward readers. *Genetic Psychology Monographs,* May 1974, *89,* 221-239.

Uses a tachistoscopic recognition to compare visual memory of 15 backward and 15 normal readers, ages 8-11, matched for age and intelligence.

COHEN, RUTH ISENBERG. Remedial training of first grade children with visual perceptual retardation. *Educational Horizons,* Winter 1966-1967, *45,* 60-63.

Analyzes pre-experimental and post-experimental scores on several measures following a 10-week visual perceptual training course for 97 boys and 58 girls who scored low on the test of visual perception and reading development and who were assigned to experimental or control groups.

COHN, MARVIN, & STRICKER, GEORGE. Inadequate perception vs. reversals. *The Reading Teacher,* November 1976, *30,* 162-167. Attempts to separate the perceptual from the cognitive issues in letter naming. Subjects were 409 children who were given a series of 12 squares, each drawn with one missing side which children had to close. All were correctly done. Children were then asked to identify letters in upper and lower case; and analyses were made of *b, d, p,* and *q* identifications. In the upper case, all except *D* were in the easiest third of the alphabet to recognize; in the lower case, all but *p* were in the hardest third to identify correctly. The authors rule out auditory discrimination as a factor in the difficulty of naming the letters and present additional evidence to support their contention that reversal errors *(b* for *d* and *d* for *b)* were not commutative or reversible. The authors concluded that no evidence was found to support the notion of consistent direction of reversal within the perception of individual children. The reversals are termed product rather than process reversals.

COHN, MARVIN, & STRICKER, GEORGE. Reversal errors in strong, average, and weak letter names. *Journal of Learning Disability,* October 1979, *12,* 533-537.
Notes the incidence of reversal errors in a letter recognition task presented to first graders and relates skill in this task to overall ability in recognizing letters in an attempt to determine the task's diagnostic value. All first grade pupils in four schools (N=409) served as subjects. Each subject was shown in a random order and asked to name all letters of the alphabet in both uppercase and lower case form. In uppercase form, the letters *B, D, P,* and *Q* ranked 3, 14, 7, and 8, respectively, in frequency of correct identification. In lower case, the respective ranks were 20, 23, 6, and 26. Lower case reversals to these four letters were examined. Of the errors made in naming the letter *p,* 35 per cent were reversals; for *b* and *d,* about 67 per cent of the errors were reversals; for *q,* 80 percent of the errors in naming were reversals. Children were then divided into thirds on the basis of letter naming ability. The poorest group named 15 or fewer letters correctly; the best group, 21 to 25 letters correctly. Analysis indicated that the highest proportion of reversal errors was made by the strong group and the lowest proportion by the weak group. Reversal errors were not found to be commutative. The authors concluded that letter reversal errors were not necessarily indicators of a basic perceptual or cognitive deficit.

COLARUSSO, RONALD P., & GILL, SALLY. Selecting a test of visual perception. *Academic Therapy,* Winter 1975-1976, *11,* 157-167.
Lists, in tabular form, age range, standardization population, time requirements, number of items, group or individual administration,

need for consumable materials, and reliability coefficients reported for 14 tests of visual functions.

COLARUSSO, RONALD P.; MARTIN, HANNAH; & HARTUNG, JOSEPH. Specific visual perceptual skills as long-term predictors of academic success. *Journal of Learning Disabilities,* December 1975, *8,* 651-655.

Estimates predictive validity of a developmental skills test administered to 57 kindergarteners and 68 first graders attending private schools in Atlanta. Subjects included 20 per cent black and were mostly middleclass. Criteria were standardized academic achievement tests administered 2 years later.

COLEMAN, JAMES C. Perceptual retardation in reading disability cases. *Journal of Educational Psychology,* December 1953, *44,* 497-503.

Summarizes the results of the nonverbal part of the Alpha Test of the Otis-Quick Scoring Tests given to 31 reading disability cases to determine if retardation in perceptual development is an important correlate of reading disability.

COOPER, J. C., JR., & GAETH, J. H. Interactions of modality with age and with meaningfulness in verbal learning. *Journal of Educational Psychology,* February 1967, *58,* 41-44.

Investigates interactions, using 932 subjects, among five grade levels (fourth, fifth, sixth, tenth, and twelfth), two modalities (auditory versus visual), and the learning of verbal materials at two levels of meaningfulness through use of a recalled paired-associate paradigm.

COPPLE, CAROL E. Effects of three variables on the performance of middle class and lower class children in discriminating similar letters in words. *The Journal of Educational Research,* February 1975, *68,* 226-229.

Compares pretests and posttests of trigram matching by 90 four-year-olds, including 10 controls, to assess the effectiveness of letter discrimination training using or not using overlays, under successive versus simultaneous presentation, on letters varying in the number of differing distinctive features.

CORNELL, EDWARD H. Identification of letter-like distortions by preschool children. *Perceptual and Motor Skills,* April 1975, *40,* 651-657.

Analyzes, in 2 studies, the characteristics of letter-like forms that facilitate their identification among 60 preschool children. Letter-like forms were generated; then distortions of these same forms were generated differing in measurable relationships (physical distances) between distortions. It was discovered that the distance relationship between distortions and particular test forms did not designate the children's choice behavior. The findings were discussed in terms of distinctive feature analysis hypotheses.

COSKY, MICHAEL J. The role of letter recognition in word recognition. *Memory and Cognition,* March 1976, *4,* 207-214.
Gathers evidence to determine if word recognition involves letter recognition by comparing the recognition latency of words composed of difficult letters with that of words composed of easy letters. Using 20 introductory psychology students, letter recognition difficulty was assessed in 2-letter discrimination tasks in which subjects were asked to make a letter/nonletter judgment on each of the 26 uppercase letters and 13 distractors in each of 8 presentations. A letter naming task was also utilized with other subjects. Fifteen subjects' visual recognition latency to 72 easy-letter words and to 72 difficult-letter words was then compared. Word frequency and length were also manipulated. Results showed no effect for letter difficulty, although there was a time decrease with word frequency and a time increase with word length. The findings suggested that letter recognition does not play a role in word recognition processes and that reading does not occur letter-by-letter.

COX, BRIAN J., & HAMBLY, LIONEL R. Guided development of perceptual skill of visual space as a factor in the achievement of primary grade children. *American Journal of Optometry and Archives of American Academy of Optometry,* August 1961, *38,* 433-444.
Reports a comparative study of change in achievement quotient of two groups of grade 2 and 3 children, one of which had 24 training sessions while the other had no training.

DAVOL, STEPHEN H., & HASTINGS, MARY LYNN. Effects of sex, age, reading ability, socio-economic level, and display position on a measure of spatial relations in children. *Perceptual and Motor Skills,* April 1967, *24,* 375-387.
Measures development in spatial relations of 96 boys and 96 girls from kindergarten through grade 3 in high, middle, and low socioeconomic classes and relates results to age, sex, reading group placement, and socioeconomic level.

DE HIRSCH, KATRINA; JANSKY, JEANNETTE J.; & LANGFORD, W. S. *Predicting Reading Failure.* New York: Harper and Row, 1966.
Calculates coefficients of correlation between assessments of environmental variables, intelligence, and test of sensorimotor, linguistic, and perceptual functioning administered to a normal group of 30 boys and 23 girls at kindergarten age, and measures of their second-grade reading achievement, and compares the findings for the normal group with findings in a similar study of 53 prematurely born subjects.

DEREVENSKY, JEFFREY L. Modal preferences and strengths: implications for reading research. *Journal of Reading Behavior,* Spring 1978, *10,* 7-23.

Gives an overview of the research findings dealing with modality preferences and strengths. The studies reviewed were categorized under: 1) visual and auditory modalities, 2) attempts to assess and identify group and individual modality preferences, and 3) attempts to match modal preference and reading instruction. Conclusions based on the research are then drawn and suggestions for areas in need of additional research are made.

DEWITZ, PETER. The process of perception in wine tasting and reading. In Malcom P. Douglass (Ed.), *Reading Between and Beyond the Lines.* Claremont Reading Conference 37th Yearbook, 1973, 156-162.

Summarizes and synthesizes the major findings from several studies on the relationship of visual perception and perceptual training to reading.

DOEHRING, D. C. Patterns of impairment in specific reading disability, a neuropsychological investigation. Bloomington, Ind.: Indiana University Press, 1968.

Compares scores on 109 measures of 39 boys, 10 to 14 years old, retarded in reading, with scores of 39 normal boys matched on age and performance IQ. Measures of sensory, motor, perceptual, and verbal abilities were statistically interrelated and compared to reading scores, neurological examinations, and case histories.

DOEHRING, DONALD G., & ROSENSTEIN, JOSEPH. Speed of visual perception in deaf children. *Journal of Speech and Hearing Research,* March 1969, *12,* 118-125.

Compares the visual perceptual speed of 50 deaf and 50 hearing children (half of whom were about 11 years old and the other half about 13 years old) equated on age, sex, and performance IQ.

DORNBUSH, RHEA L., & BASOW, SUSAN. The relationship between auditory and visual short-term memory and reading achievement. *Child Development,* 1970, *41,* 1033-1044.

Studies the relation between reading achievement and bisensory functioning in the auditory and visual modality using short-term memory as an investigative tool in a study of 72 students in grades one, three, five, and nine.

DOWNING, JOHN; AYERS, DOUGLAS; & SCHAEFER, BRIAN. Conceptual and perceptual factors in learning to read. *Educational Research,* November 1978, *21,* 11-19.

Reports the results of a structured interview conducted with 310 kindergarteners. The structured interview was conducted by 140 undergraduate education students, and each interview took 20-30 minutes. The interview had four parts: I) Recognition of acts of reading and writing; II) Concepts of the purposes of reading and writing; III) Concepts of features of printed materials; IV) Visual perception (similar to one part of the Frostig Test). Most children achieved near perfect scores on Part IV. Part I was slightly more difficult and Part III was the most difficult of all. It was concluded that teachers should be more concerned about the development of these linguistic concepts than visual perception.

DUBOIS, NELSON F. Selected correlations between reading achievement and various visual abilities of children in grades 2 and 4. *Peceptual and Motor Skills,* September 1973, *37,* 45-46.
Controls for effects of performance on verbal based tests of intellectual efficiency, then attempts to correlate various perceptual skills with reading achievement in 60 children at grades 2 and 4.

DUBOIS, NELSON F., & BROWN, FOSTER LLOYD. Selected relationships between Fostig scores and reading achievement in a first grade population. *Perceptual and Motor Skills,* October 1973, *37,* 515-519.
Assesses the ability of the Frostig test to measure skills related to reading achievement beyond those measured by 2 other reading-related tests with 163 first graders.

EAMES, THOMAS H. The relationship of the central visual field to the speed of visual perception. *American Journal of Ophthalmology,* February 1957, *63,* 279-280.
Bases conclusions on data from 50 subjects, ranging in age from 5 through 17, including measures of central fields through the use of a campimeter, and of speed of visual perception with a tachistoscope and other devices.

EDWARDS, ALLAN E. Subliminal tachistoscopic perception as a function of threshold method. *Journal of Psychology,* July 1960, *50,* 139-144.
Uses, compares, and evaluates three methods of testing thresholds of perception of words in terms of sensitivity to show the relativity of "subliminal" and "supraliminal" perception.

EGELAND, BYRON. Effects of errorless training on teaching children to discriminate letters of the alphabet. *Journal of Applied Psychology,* August 1975, *60,* 533-536.
Uses immediate and 1-week delayed posttests to compare letter discrimination of 108 preschoolers taught by errorless training with distinctive features or irrelevant cues highlighted and traditional reinforcement-extinction procedures.

EGELAND, BYRON, & WINER, KEN. Teaching children to discriminate letters of the alphabet through errorless discrimination training. *Journal of Reading Behavior*, July 1974, *6*, 143-150.

Compares the effectiveness of 2 methods of training preschoolers to discriminate between 2 letters with slightly different distinctive features. Subjects were 64 innercity children.

ELKIND, DAVID, & DEBLINGER, JO ANN. Perceptual training and reading achievement in disadvantaged children. *Child Development,* March 1969, *40,* 11-19.

Compares the reading achievement of 54 second-grade innercity black pupils on premeasures and post-measures of reading achievement and perceptual ability after 45 half-hour sessions with either a series of nonverbal perceptual exercises or a commercial reading program for urban disadvantaged, the Bank Street Readers.

ELKIND, DAVID; LARSON, MARGARET; & VAN DOORNINCK, WILLIAM. Perceptual decentration learning and performance in slow and average readers. *Journal of Educational Psychology,* February 1965, *56,* 50-56.

Tests 30 slow and 30 average readers matched on age, sex, and nonverbal IQ in grades 3 through 6 for the ability to perceive hidden figures on a set of ambiguous pictures before and after they were trained to detect such figures on another similar set.

ENGLE, RANDALL W.; CLARK, DONOVAN D.; & CATHCART, JOHN. The modality effect: is it a result of different strategies? *Journal of Verbal Learning and Verbal Behavior,* April 1980, *19,* 226-239.

Presents the results of five experiments designed to test the theory that modality effects in immediate and delayed recall are partly a result of different levels of encoding of auditory and visual recency information. All subjects were introductory psychology students. Sample sizes for the experiments varied from 72 to 148. Stimuli for all experiments were lists of words. Four of the experiments manipulated knowledge of list length and mode of presentation and found no decrement in auditory superiority when the subject was ignorant as to which items were recency items. This appears to disconfirm, in the authors' view, any theory that modality effects found for recency items in immediate free recall are a consequence of different subject strategies. Requirements for a general theory of modality effects and echoic memory were discussed.

ERICKSON, RICHARD C. Visual-haptic aptitude: effect on student achievement in reading. *Journal of Learning Disabilities,* May 1969, *2,* 256-260.

Compares the reading achievement of seventh-grade boys who were classified primarily as visual, indeterminates, and haptic (kinesthetic or tactile) perceivers.

EVANS, JAMES R. Auditory and auditory-visual integration skills as they relate to reading. *The Reading Teacher,* April 1969, *22,* 625-629.
Cites 15 sources in discussing the relationship between auditory functions and reading.

EVANS, JAMES R., & SMITH, LINDA JONES. Psycholinguistic skills of early readers. *The Reading Teacher,* October 1976, *30,* 39-43.
Studies specific psycholinguistic skills in 19 superior readers with a mean age of 5 years 8 months. The Wide Range Achievement Test was administered to assess reading ability. Additional measures included the Illinois Test of Psycholinguistic Abilities, the Bender-Gestalt Test of Visual Motor Integration, the Attention Span for Letters subtest of the Detroit Tests of Learning Aptitude, and the Colarusso-Hammill Motor-Free Test of Visual Perception. Superior readers were found to have consistently high scores in those subjects that involved short-term visual memory for letters and words and those that involved ability in sound blending. Ten additional subjects of superior intelligence, but with average ability in reading, were administered subtests of sound blending and visual memory; their scores were significantly lower than those of the superior reading groups.

FARNHAM-DIGGORY, S., & GREGG, LEE W. Short-term memory function in young readers. *Journal of Experimental Child Psychology,* April 1975, *19,* 279-298.
Compares 12 good and 12 poor grade 5 readers on tests of memory span and scanning presented both orally and visually. Relates oral reading errors to letter patterns concept assessed by subjects' construction of patterns from 4 minimally confusing letters.

FAUSTMAN, MARION N. Some effects of perception training in kindergarten on first grade success in reading. In Helen K. Smith (Ed.), *Perception and Reading,* Proceedings of the International Reading Association, *12(4),* 1968, 99-101.
Investigates the effect on first-grade reading achievement of perception training given to 14 kindergarten classes with 14 other classes as controls.

FELDMANN, SHIRLEY. Predicting early success. In J. Allen Figurel (Ed.), *Reading and Inquiry,* International Reading Association Conference Proceedings, *10,* 1965, 408-410.
Discusses the new Reading Prognosis Test which was designed to be predictive of future reading achievement as well as to give diagnostic information.

FISHER, VIRGINIA LEE. Letter discrimination as a function of culture, orthography and dimensionality of letters. *Perceptual and Motor Skills,* April 1978, *46,* 459-464.

Investigates the effect of presenting letters in a 3-dimensional display on letter discrimination among forty-six American and eighty Indian children. Two-dimensional letters were mounted on cards. Kannada (Indian) letters and English letters were randomly presented in both modes to subjects. Results indicated that more errors were made on Kannada than on English orthographic tasks, but there were relatively fewer errors made by Indian than American children. Younger subjects and boys made relatively more errors than other groups.

FORD, MARGUERITE P. Auditory-visual and tactual-visual integration in relation to reading ability. *Perceptual and Motor Skills,* June 1967, *24,* 831-841.
Correlates an auditory-visual test, tactual-visual test, intelligence test, and reading achievement measures for 121 fourth-grade boys and relates the intersensory tasks to type of reading errors made on an oral diagnostic reading test.

FORTENBERRY, W. D. An investigation of the effectiveness of a special program upon the development of visual perception for word recognition of culturally disadvantaged first grade students. In G. B. Schick & M. M. May (Eds.), *Reading: process and Pedagogy,* Nineteenth Yearbook of the National Reading Conference, 1971, *1,* 141-145.
Explores the effectiveness of visual perceptual training upon word recognition and reading achievement of 48 culturally disadvantaged first-grade pupils.

FOX, HENRY CORBETT. The relationship between the perception of tachistoscopically projected images and reading readiness. *Studies in Education*, 1952, Thesis Abstract Series, No. 4, 117-120.
Bases conclusions on comparisons of scores made by first-grade pupils at the beginning of the year on an experimental test of the perception of tachistoscopically projected images and the scores made at the end of the year on oral- and silent-reading tests.

FRIEDMAN, NATHAN. Is reading disability a fusional-eye movement disability? (Part II). *Journal of the American Optometric Association,* June 1974, *45,* 727-732.
Discusses the effects on reading of fusional eye movement training in 2 experiments with poor readers, the first with 8 ninth graders, the second comparing 40 eighth and ninth graders with a matched group of 30 given only remedial reading instruction.

FRIEDRICH, FRANCES J.; SCHADLER, MARGARET; & JUOLA, JAMES F. Developmental changes in units of processing in reading. *Journal of Experimental Child Psychology,* October 1979, *28,* 344-358. Investigates the development in facility to identify letters, syllables and words in reading normal prose. Three groups of subjects were included: 20 pupils who had completed second grade, 19 who had completed fourth grade and 20 undergraduate psychology students. The children came from predominantly white, middle-class backgrounds. The mean reading score for 16 of the 20 second graders on the Stanford Achievement Test (SAT) was 4.2, for all fourth graders it was 6.6. The stimuli were 150 nine-word sentences presented on a rear projection screen. Subjects were to find letters, syllables, words, or superordinate categories (e.g. "A Kind of Animal") in sentences. There was also a control condition of normal reading. Performance was determined by the time needed to find the target, total reading time, search errors and number of comprehension equations correctly answered (one question per sentence). Mean search time was shortest for adults and longest for second graders. Whole words were recognized significantly faster than categories, and the most slowly recognized were letters. Reading rates in the word search condition were nearly the same as normal reading rate. More comprehension errors were made in the syllable search condition. Correlation coefficients between SAT subtests and performance on the search tasks were also reported.

FROSTIG, MARIANNE. Visual modality, research and practice. In Helen K. Smith (Ed.), *Perception and Reading,* Proceedings of the International Reading Association, *12*(4), 1968, 25-33.
Relates clinical experience to published research findings in discussing symptoms of reading disabilities, visual perception disabilities, laterality motor dysfunctions, and recommended instructional procedures; cites 55 references.

FROSTIG, MARIANNE; LEFEVER, WELTY; & WHITTLESEY, JOHN. Disturbances in visual perception. *Journal of Educational Research,* November 1963, *57,* 160-162.
Reports the general results of a developmental test of visual perception given to 1,800 preschool and school children and 71 children with known or suspected neurological handicaps.

FULLER, GERALD B. Perceptual considerations in children with a reading disability. *Psychology in the Schools,* July 1964, *1,* 314-317.
Tests 287 children who ranged in age from 8 to 15 and who represented four types of readers (good, primary reading disability, secondary reading disability, and organic reader) with the Minnesota Percepto-Diagnostic Test (MPD) to ascertain whether there is a perceptual difference among various types of reading disabilities.

FULLER, GERALD B., & ENDE, RUSSELL. The effectiveness of visual perception, intelligence and reading understanding in predicting reading achievement in junior high school children. *Journal of Educational Research*, February 1967, *60*, 280-282.
Correlates reading achievement with visual perception, intelligence, and reading for understanding for 347 junior high school students from a high socioeconomic area.

GAMSKY, NEAL R., & LLOYD, FAYE WILLIAMS. A longitudinal study of visual perceptual training and reading achievement. *The Journal of Educational Research*, July-August 1971, *64*, 451-454.
Reports on the effect of visual perceptual training on the reading achievement of kindergarten pupils in 20 classes.

GEAKE, R. ROBERT. Predictors of reading rate improvement. *The interinstitutional seminar in child development, collected papers, 1962*. Dearborn, Michigan: Edison Institute, 1963, 86-93.
Studies 60 students in grades 7 through 12, organized in four groups in terms of intelligence and initial reading rate, who were given two perceptual tests before, and a reading rate test immediately after, and 15 weeks after 15 sessions of training in rapid reading to determine the relationship of intelligence, perceptual speed, and closure to reading rate improvement.

GEYER, J. J. Perceptual systems in reading: the prediction of a temporal eye-voice span. In Helen K. Smith (Ed.), *Perception and Reading*, Proceedings of the International Reading Association, 1968, *12(4)*, 44-53.
Explains a heuristic model of perception in reading and tests four hypotheses concerning temporal eye-voice span during smooth and interrupted reading. Eight subjects read three passages varying in difficulty to test the theoretical models of perception.

GEYER, L. H. Recognition and confusion of the lowercase alphabet. *Perception and Psychophysics*, November 1977, *22*, 487-490.
Estimates a visual recognition confusion matrix for the full lower case English alphabet as determined by twenty-five tachistoscopic trials per letter for each of seven male adults with normal or corrected vision. Confusion performance, averaged across stimuli and subjects, was 0.50. Subject range for accuracy of performance was 40.8 percent to 55.7 percent. A letter-by-letter tabular matrix is presented.

GIBSON, ELEANOR J. Trends in perceptual development: implications for reading process. In Anne D. Pick (Ed.), *Minnesota Symposia on Child Psychology, Volume 8*. Minneapolis: The University of Minnesota Press, 1974, 24-54.

Discusses the relationship of programmatic research findings to 3 trends in perceptual development: 1) increasing specificity of correspondence between information in stimulation and the differentiation of perception, 2) increasing optimization of attention, 3) increasing economy in the perceptual process of information pickup.

GOETZINGER, C. P. S.; DIRKS, D. D. S.; & BAER, C. J. Auditory discrimination and visual perception in good and poor readers. *Annals of Otology, Rhinology, and Laryngology,* March 1960, *69,* 121-136.

Compares 15 good with 15 poor readers, ages 10 to 12 years, equated for Binet IQs and sex, on three tests of auditory discrimination, the Raven Progressive Matrices, and two tests of visual discrimination.

GOINS, JEAN TURNER. *Visual Perceptual Abilities and Early Reading Progress.* Supplementary Educational Monographs, No. 87. Chicago: University of Chicago Press, February 1958.

Presents and analyzes data secured "1) to ascertain the level of competence in visual perception of first-grade children and the correlation of their perceptual abilities with their achievement in reading and 2) to determine the effect that training in recognition of visual forms would have on progress in learning to read."

GOLDBERG, HERMAN KRIEGER, & GUTHRIE, JOHN T. Evaluation of visual perceptual factors in reading disability. *Journal of Pediatric Ophthalmology,* February 1972, *9,* 18-25.

Presents an investigation to relate visual sequential memory and visual memory to reading in 81 normal readers (IQ 98.27), and 43 disabled readers (IQs above 80), then examines a simpler test.

GOODMAN, LIBBY, & WIEDERHOLT, J. LEE. Predicting reading achievement in disadvantaged children. *Psychology in the Schools,* April 1973, *10,* 181-184.

Compares the long-term predictive power of intelligence, readiness, achievement, and visual perception for the future reading performance of a sample of 70 innercity kindergarten and first grade children.

GORELICK, MOLLY C. The effectiveness of visual form training in a prereading program. *Journal of Educational Research,* March 1965, *58,* 315-318.

Investigates two different visual discrimination approaches to word recognition success in two experimental groups of 23 first graders each and a control group.

GREDLER, GILBERT R. Performance on a perceptual test with children from a culturally disadvantaged background. In Helen K. Smith (Ed.), *Perception and Reading,* Proceedings of the International Reading Association, *12(4),* 1968, 86-91.

Investigates the relationship between teacher rating of adjustment, achievement, and scores on the Minnesota Percepto-Diagnostic Test at third and fourth grades; results were contrasted with the performance of 15 clinic students of similar age and intelligence.

GROFF, PATRICK. Research in brief: shapes as cues to word recognition. *Visible Language,* Winter 1975, *9,* 67-71.
Discusses the concept of word shape on contours and reviews related research.

GROSS, KAREN, & ROTHENBERG, STEPHEN. An examination of methods used to test the visual perceptual deficit hypothesis of dyslexia. *Journal of Learning Disabilities,* December 1979, *12,* 670-677.
Discusses two methodological problems that often arise in dyslexia research: 1) the validity of the experimental measures and the related problem of interpreting null results and 2) the effects of sampling from a disabled population when the disorder under consideration has multiple unknown origins. The problems are illustrated through a discussion of the research aimed at testing the visual perceptual deficit hypothesis of dyslexia. Data supporting the visual perceptual deficit hypothesis are presented, and the authors suggest that this hypothesis may account for some forms of dyslexia.

GROSS, K.; ROTHENBERT, S.; SCHOTTENFELD, S.; & DRAKE, C. Duration thresholds for letter identification in left and right visuals fields for normal and reading-disabled children. *Neuropsychologia,* 1978, *16(6),* 709-714.
Examines duration thresholds for identification of letters in the right and left visual fields of twenty-nine normal and disabled readers aged 10 to 13 years. Electro-oculography monitoring of eye position was used to insure central fixation during stimulus presentation. Reading disabled subjects showed higher thresholds for stimuli in both hemifields and a greater difference between thresholds for left- and right-hemifield stimuli than normals. However, high variability among disabled readers compared to normals on the recognition task was evidenced.

GUPTA, RAJ; CECI, STEPHEN J.; & SLATER, ALAN M. Visual discrimination in good and poor readers. *Journal of Special Education,* Winter 1978, *12,* 409-416.
Describes two studies (N=24 and 26) of match-to-sample discrimination tasks performed by 7-year-old English children of average IQ, but differentiated in reading performances on the Burt Word Reading Test. In experiment 1, subjects were presented with two visual discrimination tasks: the Visual Discrimination and Orientation Test emphasizing letter strings, and a modified version of the Bender Gestalt abstract figures. In experiment 2, subjects were exposed to

three sets of stimuli: letter-like nonsense shapes, strings of letters, and pronounceable nonsense words. Results suggest match-to-sample tasks composed of unfamiliar visual forms are not differentiated by reading ability, but differences are found between good and poor readers when items to be matched are letters.

GURALNICK, MICHAEL J. Alphabet discrimination and distinctive features: research review and educational implications. *Journal of Learning Disabilities*, August/September 1972, *5*, 428-434.
Reviews literature relevant to perceptual discrimination of letters and suggests procedures to facilitate such discrimination.

HAGIN, ROSA A.; SILVER, ARCHIE A.; & HERSH, MARILYN F. Specific reading disability, teaching by stimulation of deficit perceptual areas. In J. Allen Figurel (Ed.), *Reading and Inquiry,* Proceedings of the International Reading Association, 1965, *10*, 368-370.
Compares pretest and posttest scores on a battery of perceptual and reading tests for 40 boys, ages 8 to 11 years, with reading problems and who had been paired on several variables and assigned to either an experimental group receiving 6 months of training in perceptual stimulation or a control group receiving conventional reading instruction during the same period.

HALPERN, ESTHER. Reading success by children with visual-perceptual immaturity: explorations within Piaget's theory. *American Journal of Orthopsychiatry,* March 1970, *40*, 311-312.
Deals with the cognitive compensating mechanisms of 35 second-grade children, performing below intellectual and age level expectations on two visual-perceptual tasks, in the execution of three Piagetian tasks (conservation, transivity of weight, and reliance/independence) and finds that success in reading can be predicted, for this group, at the .05 level.

HAMILTON, GEORGE E., & ANDERSON, PAUL L. Will perceptual training alone increase reading ability of adults? *The Reading Teachers' Mailbox,* No. 10. Meadville, Pennsylvania: Keystone View Company, October 1, 1956, 4-7.
Bases conclusions on the results of 26 one-half hour periods of group training through the use of the Keystone Tachistoscope and the accompanying "tachisto-slides" given to 13 stenographic and clerical women employees at the Keystone Company.

HAMMILL, D. D.; COLARUSSO, R. P.; & WIEDERHOLT, J. L. Diagnostic value of the Frostig Test: a factor analytic approach. *Journal of Special Education,* 1970, *4*, 279-282.
Ascertains whether the Frostig Developmental Test of Visual Perception subtests measure distinct areas of visual perception. The diagnostic

value of these subtests for 166 primary school disadvantaged subjects was evaluated.

HAMMILL, DONALD. Training visual perceptual processes. *Journal of Learning Disabilities*, November 1972, *5*, 552-559.
Organizes recent research to examine relationships between visual perceptions and visual perception training, and reading comprehension.

HANLEY, V., & COX, DAVID L. Individual differences in visual discrimination of letters. *Perceptual and Motor Skills*, April 1979, *48*, 539-550.
Argues that research on the distinctive features of letters has been inconclusive because the data analyses of previous studies overlooked the effect of individual variation by collapsing individual performance into group means, and because these studies employed artificial or atypical reading tasks. Ten graduate students were presented 650 letter pairs: the 325 possible "different" pairs of the 26 capital letters plus 325 "same" pairings (the letters were the same) of 12 or 13 matches of each of the 26 letters. The pairs were presented at four second intervals in blocks of 21 trials. Subjects pushed a hand-held button when they recognized the letters as different. The response latency was the dependent variable and was analyzed using INDSCAL, a multi-dimensional scaling procedure which weights individual contribution to a psychological space. The analyses yielded four underlying dimensions: linearity vs. curvature, vertical drive, angularity, and closure space. Another dimension was an artifact of the confusability of two pairs (E-F and O-Q). Individuals varied significantly in their utilization of these features, suggesting that future research must examine individual variation in the perceptual process—and that previous research should be reexamined.

HARBER, JEAN R. Are perceptual skills necessary for success in reading? Which ones? *Reading Horizons*, Fall 1979, *20*, 7-15.
Correlates performance on four tests of perception and two tests of reading for normal readers and learning disabled children. The perceptual tests were the Motor-Free Visual Perception Test, the Developmental Test of Visual-Motor Integration, and two subtests of the Illinois Test of Psycholinguistic Abilities, Sound Blending and Visual Closure. Two subtests of the Peabody Individual Attainment Test were used to measure reading: Reading Recognition and Reading Comprehension. Subjects were all tested between late October and early December of their second grade year. The 55 learning disabled children had an average IQ of 99; the 54 normal readers had an average IQ of 114. Second order partial correlation coefficients were

calculated, holding IQ and age constant. For normal readers, the intercorrelation coefficients between the perceptual and reading tests ranged from .16 to .37, and six of the eight coefficients were significant. The findings were interpreted as not supporting the view that perceptual deficits are related to reading performance in learning disabled children.

HARE, BETTY A. Perceptual deficits are not a cue to reading problems in second grade. *The Reading Teacher,* March 1977, *30,* 624-628. Hypothesizes that 81 second graders who score low on a measure of visual perception but still succeed in learning to read must have adequate or compensatory skills in audition.

HARRINGTON, SISTER MARY JAMES, & DURRELL, DONALD D. Mental maturity versus perception abilities in primary reading. *Journal of Educational Psychology,* October 1955, *46,* 375-380. Presents a summary and analysis of data secured from 1,500 second-grade pupils to determine the influence of each of the following factors on reading achievement: visual discrimination, auditory discrimination, phonics, and mental ability.

HARTLAGE, LAWRENCE C. Differential age correlates of reading ability. *Perceptual and Motor Skills,* December 1975, *41,* 968-970. Uses a reading screening instrument to examine the relationship of visual, auditory, and motor skills to reading achievement in 130 boys and girls in first, second, and third grades.

HARTUNG, JOSEPH E. Visual perceptual skills, reading ability, and the young deaf child. *Exceptional Children,* April 1970, *36,* 603-608. Evaluates the visual perceptual skills of beginning readers with normal intelligence using 30 deaf and 30 normally hearing children who were matched in chronological age, with the range being between 7.5 and 9 years.

HICKS, CAROLYN. The ITPA visual sequential memory task: an alternative interpretation and the implications for good and poor readers. *British Journal of Educational Psychology,* February 1980, *50,* 16-25. Conducts a series of four studies to determine what the Illinois Test of Psycholinguistic Abilities Visual Sequential Memory task (ITPA VSM) measures, what skills are required for adequate task performance, and how good and poor readers differ in these skills. In the first study, 20 children (mean age 9-4) who scored within the average range on the WISC and no less than three months below CA on the Schonell Graded Word Recognition Test were individually administered the VSM section of the ITPA. Each subject was asked to report his recall strategy on the VSM and performance of subjects who used a verbal labelling code was compared with performance of those who used a visual labelling code. Seven subjects reported a visual strategy and 13, a verbal strategy. The difference in the scores between the two groups was significant with subjects using a verbal labelling strategy recalling more of the visual symbols than those using a visual strategy. The findings suggested the the ITPA VSM task measures verbal encoding ability rather than visual sequential memory. The second experiment suggested that the retention of visual stimuli could be improved by adopting a verbal labelling strategy. In the third experiment, the findings suggested that when verbal labelling was suppressed, the performance of competent readers deteriorated to a level similar to that of poor readers. The results of the fourth study indicated that if retarded readers were instructed to use a verbal labelling strategy, their performance on retaining visual symbols improved significantly. The author concluded that good and poor readers may differ in their ability to employ a verbal labelling strategy rather than with respect to visual memory.

HIGBEE, KENNETH L. Recent research on visual mnemonics: historical roots and educational fruits. *Review of Educational Research,* Fall 1979, *49,* 611-629.

Reviews the research on visual mnemonics by comparing recent visual mnemonic techniques with research in the late 1800s and early 1900s. The practical education implications of recent research on mnemonics are presented.

HILL, PATRICIA J. Reversals in reading: are they abnormal? *American Journal of Optometry and Physiological Optics,* March 1980, *57,* 162-165.

Examines the prevalence and course of reversal problems from kindergarten through fourth grade. Subjects were 257 children (including some children who were placed in the junior primary grade because of lack of readiness for first grade). Fifty percent were white, 40 percent were black, and 10 percent were classified as other. Of the 257 children, 97 were referred to a special class for perceptual and motor training. Included in this referral group were 88 percent of the kindergarteners, 83 percent of the junior primary (JP) pupils, 47 percent of the first graders, 34 percent of second graders, 16 percent of third graders, and 2 percent of fourth graders. Of those referred, the percentages showing reversal tendencies were 63 percent, 80 percent, 56 percent, 53 percent, 12 percent, and 0 percent, respectively, at K, JP, and grades 1, 2, 3, and 4.

HILL, SUZANNE D., & HECKER, ELYNORDEL E. Auditory and visual learning of a paired-associate task by second grade children. *Perceptual and Motor Skills,* December 1966, *23,* 814.

Explores efficiency of paired-associate learning in visual versus auditory presentation conditions for 32 second graders who were presented, in each modality, 32 word pairs selected from preprimers.

HIRSCH, I. J. Visual and auditory perception and language learning. In F. A. Young & D. B. Lindsley (Eds.), *Early experience and visual information processing in perceptual and reading disorders*. Washington, D.C.: National Academy of Sciences, 1970, 231-243.

Discusses findings from several studies with particular emphasis on differences in reading and language between deaf and non-deaf children and studies related to stimulus mode.

HOFFMAN, LOUIS G. The relationship of basic visual skills to school readiness at the kindergarten level. *Journal of the American Optometric Association*, May 1974, *45*, 608-614.

Tests 30 kindergarten pupils to determine if a relationship exists between a set of visual skills tests and school readiness.

HUNDERI, J., & BUCHER, B. Beginning readers discriminate words by their simplest cue. *The Alberta Journal of Educational Research*, September 1977, *23*, 186-194.

Selects 12 eldest children from a group of 23 attending a university preschool as subjects in a study of visual features that are relevant in word discrimination. Subjects were trained on 3 types of artifical word lists. Each list contained 4 trigrams that varied in the complexity of the cue that could be used to discriminate among them. Lists were presented to each subject in a counter-balance sequence. The findings supported the hypothesis that in word discrimination tasks children attend to the simplest usable cue, usually a single letter, rather than those requiring use of multiple-letter cues; but the single letter cue does not aid discrimination between similar-appearing words.

HURLEY, O. L. Perceptual integration and reading problems. *Exceptional Children*, 1968, *35*, 207-215.

Investigates the relationship between reading and a battery of tests of visual-tactual-kinesthetic integration for forty matched pairs of pupils primarily from second and third grades.

HYMAN, JOAN, & COHEN, S. ALAN. The effect of verticality as a stimulus property on the letter discrimination of young children. *Journal of Learning Disabilities*, February 1975, *8*, 98-107.

Uses a matching-to-sample task to investigate the relationship between the vertical aspect of the letter and the number of reversals. Subjects were 180 randomly selected kindergarteners who were randomly assigned to one of 4 tasks: 1) matching letters containing both vertical and directional aspects *(p* to *p, b, d, g)*; 2) matching letters containing directional aspects only (*c* to *c, u, n*); 3) matching Task 1 letters with strength of the vertical element reduced; and 4) matching Task 1 letters with the strength of the directional aspect reduced. The verticality aspect of the stimulus figure interfered with subjects' performance even more than directionality.

JACOBS, JAMES N. An evaluation of the Frostig visual-perceptual training program. *Educational Leadership*, January 1968, *25*, 332-340.
Analyzes the effect of training with the Frostig program on performance on the Frostig test and on reading readiness for two prekindergarten, two kindergarten, and two first-grade classes.

JACOBS, JAMES N.; WIRTHLIN, LENORE D.; & MILLER, CHARLES B. A follow-up evaluation of the Frostig visual-perceptual training program. *Educational Leadership*, November 1968, *26*, 169-175.
Attempts to answer questions related to the predictive validity of a visual-perceptual test and the cumulative effect of the Frostig program on reading achievement by evaluating the over 300 prekindergarten, kindergarten, and first- and second-grade children in the study.

JESTER, ROBERT E. Comments on Hsia's auditory, visual, and audiovisual information processing. *Journal of Communications*, December 1968, *18*, 346-349.
Measures comprehension of three forms of a reading test given to subjects at varying rates in an auditory, visual, and audiovisual presentation and establishes relationships within and between presentation conditions.

JESTER, ROBERT E., & TRAVERS, ROBERT M. W. Comprehension of connected meaningful discourse as a function of rate and mode of presentation. *Journal of Educational Research*, March 1966, *59*, 297-302.
Compares the comprehension of 15 groups totaling 220 college students to eight passages administered to each group at either one of five speeds through either the visual, the auditory, or the audiovisual modality of presentation.

JUOLA, JAMES F.; SCHADLER, MARGARET; CHABOT, ROBERT J.; & MCCAUGHEY, MARK W. The development of visual information processing skills related to reading. *Journal of Experimental Child Psychology*, June 1978, *25*, 459-476.
Assesses the proficiency with which a total of eighty subjects at various ages engage in a visual search task. Included in the study were twenty subjects from each of the following age/grade levels: kindergarten, second grade, fourth grade, and college/adult. The

search task consisted of the visual presentation of a target letter followed by a 3-, 4-, or 5-letter display. The target letter was included in the display on half the trials, and the displays were comprised of common words, orthographically regular pseudowords, and irregular non-words. While response times decreased with age, the three oldest groups showed similar effects for the size and structure of the displays. Response times increased linearly with the number of display letters, and responses were faster for word and pseudoword displays than for nonwords. Kindergarteners utilized a different search strategy in which they did not differentiate among the various types of letter/word displays.

KAHN, DALE & BIRCH, HERBERT G. Development of auditory-visual integration and reading achievement. *Perceptual and Motor Skills,* October 1968, *27,* 459-468.
Studies the interrelationships among auditory-visual integrative competence, IQ, and type of reading task for 350 boys in grades 2 through 6.

KAK, ANITA, & BROWN, DONALD R. Visual pattern perception: a multidimensional analysis of development of children's reading skills. *Perceptual and Motor Skills,* December 1979, *49,* 819-830.
Compares the visual pattern recognition skills of good and poor readers at four grade levels. Stimuli were selected to reflect the major features of the alphabet. There were 12 stimuli: a single line, a single right angle, and a single arc, each presented in four degrees of rotation or directions. The 12 stimuli patterns were combined into the 66 possible pairs and each pair was used to construct 6 three-choice oddity problems, formed by designating one pattern as correct and repeating the other pattern. These patterns were presented on a rear projection screen. Each problem was presented twice. Discrimination latency was the independent variable. On the basis of the Metropolitan Readiness Tests or the Stanford Achievement Test, six good and six poor readers were selected from each of grades kindergarten, 1, 2, and 3. It was reported that all children had normal intelligence as measured on the Slosson Intelligence Test. Data were analyzed with analysis of variance and multidimensional scaling techniques. Good readers were more efficient than poor readers at all four grades. Poor readers became significantly more efficient over time. Also, there was no evidence that relations among the patterns were perceived to be different by poor readers at any age. There was a great deal of similarity across ages and between good and poor readers; no pattern-specific effects discriminated good from poor readers. The authors concluded that the differences between good and poor readers at these ages cannot be attributed to differences in processing spatial information.

KAMPWIRTH, THOMAS J., & BATES, MARION. Modality preference and teaching method: a review of the research. *Academic Therapy,* May 1980, *15,* 597-605.
Discusses 22 studies which have investigated the modalities methods problem with children under ten years of age. The article concluded that there is little evidence supporting the efficacy of matching preferred modality to teaching approach.

KATZ, PHYLLIS A. Verbal discrimination performance of disadvantaged children: stimulus and subject variables. *Child Development,* March 1967, *38,* 233-242.
Compares discrimination performance on visual and auditory tasks presented in both Hebrew and English to 72 black males of differing reading achievement levels in grades 2, 4, and 6.

KATZ, PHYLLIS A., & DEUTSCH, MARTIN. Modality of stimulus presentation in serial learning for retarded and normal readers. *Perceptual and Motor Skills,* October 1964, *19,* 627-633.
Uses a sample of 48 black males in first, third, and fifth grades to explore auditory and visual learning efficiency and its relationship to both age and reading proficiency.

KEOGH, BARBARA K. Optometric vision training programs for children with learning disabilities: review of issues and research. *Journal of Learning Disabilities,* April 1974, *7,* 219-231.
Summarizes research related to the effects of vision training programs used to enhance readiness skills and for remediation of learning problems.

KERSHNER, JOHN R. Visual-spatial organization and reading: support for a cognitive-developmental interpretation. *Journal of Learning Disabilities,* January 1975, *8,* 37-43.
Compares the effectiveness of 2 conceptually different tests of visualization to differentiate good and poor readers in one second grade containing 20 middleclass children.

KING, ETHEL M. Effects of different kinds of visual discrimination training on learning to read words. *Journal of Educational Psychology,* December 1964, *55,* 325-333.
Compares learning performances of six groups (23 each) of kindergarten pupils in ability to recognize four words following different types of stimuli and methods of presentation of visual discrimination tasks.

KING, ETHEL M. Learning to read words: An experiment in visual discrimination. In J. Allen Figurel (Ed.), *Reading and Inquiry,* International Reading Association Conference Proceedings, 10, 1965, 337-340.

Presents a research study on determining the effects of visual discrimination training with different types of stimulus materials and different methods of stimulus presentation.

KING, ETHEL M., & MUEHL, SIEGMAR. Effects of visual discrimination training on immediate and delayed word recognition in kindergarten children. *Alberta Journal of Educational Research*, June 1971, *17*, 77-87.
Presents evidence on the relative effectiveness of five different kinds of visual discrimination training on the ability of 160 kindergarteners to recall words similar or dissimilar in configuration and sound.

KIRSNER, KIM. Developmental changes in short-term recognition memory. *British Journal of Psychology*, February 1972, *63*, 109-117.
Uses naming and recognition latencies to discover whether differences exist between auditory and visual presentations and retrieval of items in short-term memory. Sixteen subjects from each age range (9-10, 13-14, 18-32, 51-69) participated.

KOLERS, P. A., & PERKINS, D. N. Orientation of letters and their speed of recognition. *Perception and Psychophysics*, 1969, *5*, 275-280.
Investigates the influence of the direction of the scan and the orientation of letters on naming letters individually or in groups. Ten right-handed male undergraduates were tested in two sessions held on different days.

KRAUSEN, R. The relationship of certain pre-reading skills to general ability and social calls in nursery children. *Educational Research*, November 1972, *15*, 72-79.
Examines the extent to which skills of visual perception are related to language, general ability, and occupation of parents in 160 preschool children, ages 3 to 5.

LAHEY, BENJAMIN B., & LEFTON, LESTER A. Discrimination of letter combinations in good and poor readers. *Journal of Special Education*, Summer 1976, *10*, 205-210.
Compares, in 2 experiments, the performance of randomly selected good and poor readers on an untimed match-to-sample task involving letter combinations of different lengths. The two 60-pupil samples included children from grades 2, 3, and 5. Children made more matching errors where several letters rather than one letter were involved. Poor readers made more errors than good readers on longer items. A decline in number of errors was found with increasing grade level.

LAHEY, BENJAMIN B., & MCNEES, M. PATRICK. Letter-discrimination errors in kindergarten through third grade: assessment and operant training. *The Journal of Special Education,* Summer 1975, *9,* 191-199.
Considers the problem of training perceptual skills in young children through a behavioral perspective. Includes a normative study with a sample of 200 from kindergarten to third grade and a sample of 29 low income preschool children in a training experiment.

LAPRAY, MARGARET HELEN, & ROSS, RAMON. Auditory and visual perceptual training. In J. Allen Figurel (Ed.), *Vistas in Reading,* International Reading Association Conference Proceedings, 11(1), 1966, 530-532.
Offers background and three suggestions for teachers wishing to do a better job in developing reading readiness.

LARSEN, STEPHEN C.; ROGERS, DOROTHY; & SOWELL, VIRGINIA. The use of selected perceptual tests in differentiating between normal and learning disabled children. *Journal of Learning Disabilities,* February 1976, *9,* 85-90.
Administers a variety of diagnostic perceptual tests to 30 normal and 59 learning disabled children entering fourth grade. All subjects were judged to be of normal intelligence; LD subjects ranged from 1 to 2 grade levels below grade placement in reading on the Stanford Reading Achievement Test. Subjects were administered the Auditory and Visual Sequential Memory and Sound Blending subtests of the Illinois Test of Psycholinguistic Abilities, the Wepman Auditory Discrimination Test, and the Bender Visual-Motor Gestalt Test (BVMG). Only the BVMG significantly differentiated normals and LDs; LD children tended to score higher than normals on all other perceptual measures. Additionally, there were no significant differences between severely and mildly reading retarded subjects on any of the measures.

LEIBERT, R. E., & SHERK, J. K. Three Frostig visual perception subtests and specific reading tasks for kindergarten, first, and second grade children. *The Reading Teacher,* 1970, *24,* 130-137.
Compares the performance of primary school children on Frostig's subtests of Position in Space, Spatial Relations, and Figure Ground with performance on tests of letter discrimination, word discrimination, phrase discrimination, and word identification.

LEIDER, ALICE B. Relationship of visual perception to word discrimination. In Helen M. Robinson and Helen K. Smith (Eds.), *Clinical Studies in Reading III,* Supplementary Educational Monographs, 97, 1968, 104-108.
Calculates intercorrelation coefficients to determine relationship among scores on three tests of visual perception, two forms of a word

discrimination test, an achievement and an intelligence test, given to 70 pupils in grade 4.

LILLY, M. STEPHEN, & KELLEHER, JOHN. Modality strengths and aptitude-treatment interaction. *The Journal of Special Education,* Spring 1973, *7,* 5-13.
Develops a test of visual and auditory memory and relates it to the reading and listening performance of 57 learning disabled children between 8 and 12 years old.

LINDER, R., & FILLMER, H. T. Auditory and visual performance of slow readers. *The Reading Teacher,* 1970, *24,* 17-22.
Compares the effectiveness of auditory, visual, and simultaneous auditory-visual presentations to 108 second-grade southern black boys.

LLOYD, BRUCE A. The relationship between visual-tactual training and children's reading achievement and mental maturity, a small sample study. *Journal of the Reading Specialist,* March 1966, *3,* 108-112.
Investigates relationships between pretraining and post-training scores on measures of visual-tactual ability, mental maturity, and reading achievement for 10 reading clinic clients, aged 9 to 15, who received perceptual training and remedial reading during 17 weeks.

LOCKHARD, JOAN, & SIDOWSKI, JOSEPH B. Learning in fourth and sixth graders as a function of sensory mode of stimulus presentation and overt or covert practice. *Journal of Educational Psychology,* October 1961, *52,* 262-265.
Seeks to determine the influence of three modes of presentation (auditory, visual, and auditory-visual) and two modes of responding (overt and covert) on 18 grade 4 and 18 grade 6 pupils who learned lists of nonsense syllables.

LOVEGROVE, WILLIAM; BILLING, GRAHAM; & SLAGHUIS, WALTER. Processing of visual contour orientation information in normal and disabled reading children. *Cortex,* June 1978, *14,* 268-278.
Compares the processing of visual contour orientation information in normal and disabled readers. Subjects in all of the four experiments conducted were 14 disabled readers and 14 matched controls. Matching was done on IQ, as measured by the WISC and reading ability, as measured by the Neale Analysis of Reading Ability, the Schonell Diagnostic Attainment Reading Test and the Word Recognition Test. The disabled readers were at least 2.5 years below grade level in reading. The average age of both groups was 9.8. Stimuli for the four experiments were lines presented in various formats and at various orientations on a three-field Scientific Prototype tachistoscope. On the first two experiments, reading disabled students had significantly longer visual information store durations than controls, and Experi-

ment 4 results indicated that good and poor readers also differed in their processing of information in the visual cortex.

LOVELL, K., & GORTON, A. A study of some differences between backward and normal readers of average intelligence. *British Journal of Educational Psychology,* 1968, *38,* 240-248.
Compares scores of fifty disabled and fifty normal nine- to ten-year-olds on a battery of ten visuo-spatial and neuropsychological tests. Intercorrelations and a factor analysis were performed for each group to determine whether reading age could be classified by score patterns indicative of neurological impairment.

LUPKER, STEPHEN J. On the nature of perceptual information during letter perception. *Perception and Psychophysics,* April 1979, *25,* 303-312.
Investigates the role and the identities of the features of letters used in letter recognition, specifically, the build up of perceptual information during the perceptual process. Discusses the feature accumulation and global-to-local models of letter perception. The stimuli for the experiment conducted were blurred images created by defocusing a slide. Subjects were 11 volunteer University of Wisconsin undergraduates. Stimulus, response and interstimulus interval were recorded. A simple masking paradigm was used. Subjects' responses were first to name the feature (letter, lines, non-words), then one of the four specific stimuli of that feature. The results were not in line with the predictions of feature accumulation models, but were predicted by a global-to-local model. The author hypothesized that when a letter is presented, the observer initially perceives a large array of information and then the perceptual system brings the letter into focus.

MACKINNON, G.E., & MCCARTHY, NANCY A. Verbal labelling, auditory-visual integration, and reading ability. *Canadian Journal of Behavioral Science,* April 1973, *5,* 124-132.
Examines performance of 32 second-grade boys on a verbal labelling (paired associate) and on auditory-visual integration tasks, then analyzes relationships among these scores, reading, and IQ scores.

MACKWORTH, JANE F., & MACKWORTH, N. H. How children read: matching by sight and sound. *Journal of Reading Behavior,* September 1974, *6,* 295-303.
Investigates relationships between reading achievement and matching for visual or auditory similarity using pairs of upper and lower case letters, homophones, and pictures. Over 70 children ages 7 to 12 participated.

MARCEL, TONY, & RAJAN, PAUL. Lateral specialization for recognition of words and faces in good and poor readers. *Neuropsychologia,* October 1975, *13,* 489-497.

Investigates perception of words and faces presented unilaterally to the right or left visual field in 20 boys and 20 girls, ages 7 to 9. Subjects were divided into good and poor readers on the basis of the Schonell test and the National Foundation for Educational Research Reading Test. All subjects were determined to be both right-handed and right-footed. Subjects were presented with 5-letter words in one session and with photographs of male faces in a second session held one week later. On the word task, good readers showed greater right-field superiority than poor readers. On the face task, a left visual field superiority was demonstrated; but this was not related to reading ability. The authors conclude that the development of hemispheric specialization for verbal processing is unrelated to that for visuo-spatial processing.

MARCHBANKS, GABRIELLE, & LEVIN, HARRY. Cues by which children recognize words. *Journal of Educational Psychology,* April 1965, *56,* 57-61.

Attempts to discover the cues by which children recognize three- and five-letter words by studying 50 kindergarten and 50 first-grade children who were required to select from a group of pseudo-words, the one similar to a word that had just been exposed to them.

MARGOLIS, HOWARD. Relationship between auditory-visual integration, reading readiness, and conceptual tempo. *The Journal of Psychology,* July 1976, *93,* 181-189.

Studies the relationship between specific perceptual skills and general reading readiness test performance with 82 kindergartners. Correlations were calculated between a modified version of the Birch and Belmont auditory-visual integration test and the Metropolitan Readiness Test (MRT). Sub-samples of subjects were also identified as impulsive or reflective on the basis of the Matching Familiar Figures Tests; these subjects were also administered the Wechsler Preschool and Primary Scale of Intelligence (WPPSI). Auditory-visual integration variance accounted for 29 percent of the variance in MRT scores. Reflectives performed significantly better in auditory-visual integration than impulsives with or without WPPSI Verbal IQ or response time held constant. However, although the impulsive pupils scored significantly better on the MRT, this did not hold true when scores were equated for WPPSI Verbal IQ.

MASON, GEORGE E., & WOODCOCK, CARROLL. First graders' performance on a visual memory for words task. *Elementary English,* September 1973, *50,* 865-870.
Determines the methods used by 2 first grade classes to match word forms held in short-term memory.

MCANINCH, MYRENE. Identification of visual perceptual errors in young children. In J. Allen Figurel (Ed.), *Vistas in Reading,* International Reading Association Conference Proceedings, 11(1), 1966, 507-512.
Questions whether or not current testing instruments reliably measure skills relevant to the reading process.

MCINTYRE, CURTIS W.; MURRAY, MICHAEL E.; CRONIN, CARMODY M.; & BLACKWELL, SCOTT L. Span of apprehension in learning disabled boys. *Journal of Learning Disabilities,* October 1978, *11,* 468-475.
Compares the influence of visual interference upon the forced-choice letter recognition (span of apprehension) for two groups of boys, 6 to 11 years old, of normal intelligence, twenty of whom were diagnosed as "learning disabled" by a multi-test battery and a matching sample of twenty normal progress learners. With no interference, apprehension span was equivalent between groups. Presence of visual noise reduced span more notably for learning disabled boys. Physical similarity of letter distractors did not distinguish between groups.

MCKEEVER, WALTER F., & VANDEVENTER, ALLAN D. Dyslexic adolescents: evidence of impaired visual and auditory language processing associated with normal lateralization and visual responsivity. *Cortex,* December 1975, *11,* 361-378.
Reports results of 2 experiments conducted a year apart on 9 dyslexic and 9 non-dyslexic controls, all right-handed adolescents attending a reading clinic. Subjects were compared on memory for binocular and dichotic stimuli and laterality. Tasks given in the first experiment were unilateral and bilateral tachistoscopic word recognitions and a tachistoscopic recognition report-time task for single lateralized letter stimuli. In the second experiment, the same tasks were readministered with modifications and dichotic digits and motor reaction time-stimulus detection tasks were added. Dyslexics were found to 1) possess left hemisphere language specialization; 2) show normal interhemispheric processing delays for single letter stimuli; 3) be impaired in their efficiency of visual and auditory processing of simple language stimuli; 4) possess clear auditory memory deficits for verbal material; and 5) possibly possess an additional deficit of left hemisphere visual association area function.

MILLER, LEON K., & TURNER, SUZANNE. Development of hemifield differences in word recognition. *Journal of Educational Psychology,* October 1973, *65,* 172-176.
Studies 15 subjects at each of 4 grade levels—second, fourth, sixth, and college—in terms of preceptual laterality development, then correlates these data with reading achievement, word recognition, and chronological age.

MILLOY, DOUGLAS G. Comment on recognition and confusion of the lowercase alphabet. *Perception and Psychophysics,* August 1978, *24,* 190-191.
Criticizes a previous analysis of a full alphabet confusion matrix for lowercase letters in foveal vision.

MORENCY, ANNE. Auditory modality, research and practice. In Helen K. Smith (Ed.), *Perception and Reading,* Proceedings of the International Reading Association, *12(4),* 1968, 17-21.
Presents findings from a longitudinal study of 179 pupils which investigated the development of auditory discrimination and visual memory and their relationship to one another and to reading achievement.

MORENCY, ANNE, & WEPMAN, JOSEPH M. Early perceptual ability and later school achievement. *The Elementary School Journal,* March 1973, *73,* 323-327.
Studies the relationship between auditory and visual perception tests administered in grade 1 and achievement in grades 4, 5, and 6 for 120 children.

MORRISON, FREDERICK J.; GIORDANI, BRUNO; & NAGY, JILL. Reading disability: an information-processing analysis. *Science,* April 1977, *196,* 77-79.
Compares the relative influence of perceptual and memory disorders on reading disability for 2 groups of 12-year-old boys identified as either normal readers or poor readers. Poor readers were identified as having at least a 2-year deficit in reading according to the Comprehensive Test of Basic Skills; poor readers were also of at least average intelligence, evidencing no sign of gross behavioral or organic disorders. The experimental task consisted of measuring recognition thresholds of good and poor readers for 3 sets of figures differing in degree of familiarity: letters, geometric forms, and abstract forms. It was hypothesized that if reading disability were a perceptual deficit, then poor readers would be inferior in recognition time to normals at short delays (0 to 300 msecs.). However, if reading disability involved an encoding or memory deficit, performance of poor readers would be inferior only at later intervals (after 300 msecs.

delay). Results indicated no differences between good and poor readers across 0 to 300 msecs. delay intervals, regardless of type of stimulus material. However, normals did perform significantly better than disabled readers during the encoding-memory phase; this superiority held for all 3 sets of stimuli. The authors argue that poor readers show some problem in processing information following initial perception.

MORTENSON, W. P. Selected pre-reading tasks, socioeconomic status, and sex. *The Reading Teacher,* 1968, *22,* 45-49, 61.
Analyzes mean scores of 1,500 first-grade boys and girls on eight auditory and visual discrimination tasks and on an IQ test administered in the second grade. Socioeconomic levels and sex were the independent variables.

MUEHL, SIEGMAR. The effects of visual discrimination pretraining on learning to read a vocabulary list in kindergarten children. *Journal of Educational Psychology,* August 1960, *51,* 217-221.
Reports an experiment which "compared the performance of three groups of kindergarten children in learning to read a vocabulary test"; the groups differed in the type of visual discrimination pretraining given before the learning task and the stimuli for each group were the same words that appeared in the vocabulary list, different words, and geometric forms.

MUEHL, SIEGMAR. The effects of visual discrimination pretraining with word and letter stimuli on learning to read a word list in kindergarten children. *Journal of Educational Psychology,* August 1961, *52,* 215-221.
Compares transfer to the reading task from pretraining in discrimination with words among three groups of children who received pretraining in which: 1) both shape and letter differences were relevant to the final task, 2) only letter differences were pertinent, and 3) relevant letters only were pertinent.

MUEHL, SIEGMAR, & KING, ETHEL M. Recent research in visual discrimination—significance for beginning reading. In J. A. Figurel (Ed.), *Vistas in Reading,* International Reading Association Conference Proceedings, 11(1), 1966, 434-439.
Reviews research concerning how children discriminate visually among words and suggests some implications for teaching; cites 15 sources.

NELSON, ROSEMARY O., & WEIN, KENNETH S. Training letter discrimination by presentation of high-confusion versus low-confusion alternatives. *Journal of Educational Psychology,* December 1974, *66,* 926-931.

Uses match-to-sample tasks to teach preschoolers (N = 8 per group) letter discrimination. Compares groups trained on similar, dissimilar, and no-letters on trials to criterion and posttest gains.

NELSON, ROSEMARY O., & WEIN, KENNETH S. The use of varying high-confusion versus low-confusion sequences to teach letter discrimination. *Journal of Reading Behavior,* Summer 1976, *8,* 161-171.
Focuses on 3 different types of matching-to-sample-letter discrimination tasks to determine which one best facilitated letter recognition in reading. The sample consisted of 28 preschool children, ages 2 and a half to 4 and a half years. Employed were letter discrimination training of high-confusion alternatives, low-confusion alternatives, or a sequence of low-, middle-, and high-confusion alternatives. On posttest 1, given after a criterion of 2 consecutive errorless training days, only the high-confusion and sequence groups signficantly improved over their pretest scores as compared with the no-treatment control group. On posttest 2, however, given after a standard number of 20 training days, the performance of all 3 training groups, including low-confusion, was superior to the performance of the controls; no differences were found among the 3 training groups.

NODINE, C. F., & HARDT, J. V. Role of letter-position cues in learning to read words. *Journal of Educational Psychology,* 1970, *61,* 10-15.
Studies the ability of 64 prereading children ranging in age from 5-3 to 6-5 years to differentiate among high and low confusion of letter pairs encountered in pseudoword context.

NOLAND, EUNICE C., & SCHULDT, W. Sustained attention and reading retardation. *Journal of Experimental Education,* Winter 1971, *40(2),* 73-76.
Compares the ability of 20 fourth-grade retarded readers to sustain visual attention with that of 20 normal readers.

O'CONNOR, WILLIAM J. The relationship between the Bender-Gestalt Test and the Marianne Frostig Developmental Test of Visual Perception. In. G. D. Spache (Ed.), *Reading Disability and Perception,* International Reading Association Conference Proceedings, 13, 1969, 72-81.
Explores the relationship between tests of visual-motor perception, intelligence, and reading readiness, in terms of age, sex, intelligence, and socioeconomic status using 89 first- and second-grade children from middle and lower socioeconomic class levels.

OLIVER, PETER R.; NELSON, JACQUELYN M.; & DOWNING, JOHN. Differentiation of grapheme-phoneme units as a function of orthography. *Journal of Educational Psychology,* October 1972, *63,* 487-491.

Examines the ability of 20 male and 20 female kindergarten children to visually differentiate the graphemic structure of words, using 4 different orthographies.

OLSON, A. V., & JOHNSON, C. I. Structure and predictive validity of the Frostig Developmental Test of Visual Perception in grades one and three. *Journal of Special Education*, 1970, *4*, 49-52.
Determines if the Frostig Development Test of Visual Perception measures several different perceptual abilities and also how well the test predicts reading achievement at first and third grades.

OLSON, ARTHUR V. The Frostig Developmental Test of Visual Perception as a predictor of specific reading abilities with second-grade children. *Elementary English*, December 1966, *43*, 869-872.
Presents an intercorrelation matrix indicating relationships among subtest and total scores on the Frostig instrument and nine measures, six of which were designed to reveal reading difficulty, for 29 girls and 42 boys in second grade.

OLSON, ARTHUR V. Relation of achievement test scores and specific reading abilities to the Frostig Developmental Test of Visual Perception. *Perceptual and Motor Skills*, February 1966, *22*, 179-184.
Reports the correlations between the scores of 71 second-grade children on the Frostig Test of Visual Perception and a battery of tests measuring intelligence, achievement, and specific reading abilities.

OLSON, ARTHUR V. School achievement, reading ability, and specific visual perception skills in the third grade. *The Reading Teacher*, April 1966, *19*, 490-492.
Correlates the scores of 121 third-grade pupils on a battery of reading and achievement tests with their scores on the Frostig Development Test of Visual Perception.

OLSON, JACK R. A factor analytic study of the relation between the speed of visual perception and the language abilities of deaf adolescents. *Journal of Speech and Hearing*, June 1967, *10*, 354-360.
Correlates five visual perceptual tests and three language measures for 20 male and 19 female deaf subjects, ages 12 to 16 years, and factor-analyzes the resulting data.

O'NEILL, G., & STANLEY, G. Visual processing of straight lines in dyslexic and normal children. *British Journal of Educational Psychology*, November 1976, *46*, 323-327.
Compares dyslexics to non-dyslexics on a pair of perceptual tasks. A total of 26 subjects, with an average age of 12 years, participated in the

experiment. Criteria for judging dyslexics included a 2.5 year deficit in reading, average or above performance on the Progressive Matrices 38, average or above performance in other classes, and no gross behavioral or organic dysfunctions. In Experiment 1, subjects were presented with a line perceptual display; portions of the display were presented to the right visual channel, while the rest of the display was presented to the left. Some perceptual displays were spatially overlapped, while others were not; the task was to identify whether 1 or 2 lines appeared in the display. Dyslexics as a group had about a 10 to 15 msec. longer separation time than normals. In a second experiment, single straight line contours were preceded by a homogeneous light mask. Dyslexics, again, required longer stimulus exposures for detection than controls. The authors hold that their findings support the view of a developmental lag in the visual information processing of dyslexics.

OTTO, WAYNE. Ability of poor readers to discriminate paired associates under differing conditions of confirmation. *Journal of Educational Research,* April 1963, *56,* 428-431.
Makes an evaluation of the difficulty of 30 poor readers from grades 4 to 7, 10 being assigned to each of three modes of reinforcement (visual, auditory, and kinaesthetic), in learning a list of paired associates (geometric forms and nonsense syllables) and explores reasons for ease or difficulty of association.

OTTO, WAYNE. The acquisition and retention of paired associates by good, average, and poor readers. *Journal of Educational Psychology,* October 1961, *52,* 241-248.
Makes an evaluation of the effects of three levels of reading achievement (good, average, and poor) with three levels of grade placement (2, 4, and 6) and three modes of reinforcement (visual, auditory, and kinesthetic) on learning a list of paired associates, consisting of geometric forms and nonsense syllables, as well as on retention and relearning after 24 hours.

PARADIS, EDWARD E. The appropriateness of visual discrimination exercises in reading readiness materials. *The Journal of Educational Research,* February 1974, *67,* 276-278.
Investigates the abilities of 119 preschoolers and 440 kindergarten students with reading readiness exercises.

PICK, ANNE D. Perception in the acquisition of reading. In Frank B. Murray & John J. Pikulski (Eds.), *The acquisition of reading: cognitive, linguistic, and perceptual prerequisites.* Baltimore: University Park Press, 1978, 99-122.
Argues that research on the perceptual components of reading suffers from lack of a conceptual analysis of the reading task that has

ecological validity. Describes a number of perceptual models of reading and presents results of research.

PICK, ANNE D. Some basic perceptual processes in reading. *Young Children,* January 1970, *25,* 162-181.

Evaluates 58 available research studies in terms of their success in identifying the basic perceptual processes in reading and specifies some of the reasons for the success or failure of the studies in attaining this goal.

PIKULSKI, JOHN J. Critique: translating research in perception and reading into practice. In Frank B. Murray & John J. Pikulski (Eds.), *The acquisition of reading: cognitive, linguistic, and perceptual prerequisites.* Baltimore: University Park Press, 1978, 123-130.

Examines the gap between reading researchers and practitioners and betweeen research and practice with special reference to the field of perceptual processes in reading. Related research is included.

PITCHER-BAKER, GEORGIA. The Rosetta Stone revisited, or...? *Academic Therapy,* Fall 1976, *12,* 39-51.

Summarizes and evaluates 5 studies which examine the effects of perceptual training on reading.

POPP, HELEN M. The measurement and training of visual discrimination skills prior to reading instruction. *Journal of Experimental Education,* Spring 1967, *35,* 15-26.

Investigates effects of test-specific discrimination training with 127 beginning first graders who were pretested for visual discrimination of bigrams and trigrams and assigned either to the experimental group which received test-specific discrimination training or to the control group which received nontest specific discrimination training.

POPP, HELEN M. Visual discrimination of alphabet letters. *The Reading Teacher,* January 1964, *17,* 221-226.

Establishes the relative difficulty of the visual discrimination of letters by presenting, by means of a modified slide projector, to 65 kindergarten children (aged 5.1 to 6.1) two alternative alphabet letter stimuli to match with a sample letter.

POTTER, MURIEL CATHERINE. *Perception of Symbol Orientation and Early Reading Success.* Contributions to Education No. 939. New York: Bureau of Publications, Teachers College, Columbia University, 1949.

Analyzes the results of tests given to 176 first-grade children to determine the extent of occurrence among them of "errors in visual perception which have been found characteristic of children who fail to progress at the expected rate in the acquisition of reading skill."

RAYNER, KEITH. Developmental changes in word recognition strategies. *Journal of Educational Psychology,* June 1976, *68,* 323-329. Deals with developmental changes in children's ability to process the graphological features of letter positions and word shape. Subjects were 144 kindergarten through sixth grade children, 18 at each grade level. In addition, 18 undergraduate college students participated. All elementary children were from the upper one-fourth of their school as identified by the reading test scores and all scores at least one-year above grade level. Mean IQs ranged from 121 to 126. Subjects were presented with artifically constructed words in the form of trigrams, quadrigrams, and quingrams and asked to select an alternative most resembling it. Subjects could respond on the basis of individual letter position and overall word shape. With increasing age, same-shape alternatives were chosen more frequently. First letter position was selected most frequently through second grade but levelled off between grades 2 through 4, followed by a decrease in the frequency of choosing the first letter beginning with grade 5.

RICHARDSON, ELLIS; DIBENEDETTO, BARBARA; CHRIST, ADOLPH; & PRESS, MARK. Relationship of auditory and visual skills to reading retardation. *Journal of Learning Disabilities,* February 1980, *13,* 77-82. Correlates performance on six measures of visual and auditory perception with reading performance. The subjects tested were 77 Brooklyn children in grades two to six whose names had been submitted to the Learning Center at Downstate Medical Center for a special reading project. There were 46 boys and 31 girls with an average age of 10-0 and an average WISC IQ of 82. All came from families with incomes below $12,000. There were 33 black and 44 white children. Five subtests of the ITPA (three auditory subtests and two visual) and the Beery Developmental Test of Visual-Motor Integration were administered. Specific sight-word and phonic reading skills and oral reading were measured by: the Roswell-Chall Diagnostic Reading Test, the Englemann-Becker Corrective Reading Placement Test, the Reading Recognition Test of the Peabody Individual Achievement Test, Boder's Informal Word Recognition Inventory, and the Gilmore Oral Reading Test. Partial correlation coefficients (controlling for age and IQ) between auditory perception and reading ranged from .00 to .51, and between visual perception and reading, from -.20 to .29. It was concluded that the findings did not support the hypothesis that children can be sorted successfully into auditory and visual learner categories with instruments used.

RICHARDSON, J. A factorial analysis of reading ability in 10-year-old primary school children. *British Journal of Educational Psychology,* November 1950, *20,* 200-201.

Summarizes briefly the results of a factorial analysis based on the responses of 260 children to a battery of 21 tests (reading, language, visual and auditory discrimination) and "assessments of experimental background and of attitude to reading."

RITTER, DAVID R., & SABATINO, DAVID A. The effects of method of measurement upon children's performance on visual perceptual tasks. *Journal of School Psychology,* Winter 1974, *12,* 296-304.
Uses multi-trait (figure-ground perception and form discrimination), multi-method (naming and recognition of stimuli presented tachistoscopically and untimed) matrix analysis to determine the contribution of trait and method to test scores of 64 first graders with average or above average intelligence.

ROBERTS, RICHARD W., & COLEMAN, JAMES C. An investigation of the role of visual and kinesthetic factors in reading failure. *Journal of Educational Research,* February 1958, *51,* 445-451.
Presents the results of a controlled experiment involving 27 boys in the experimental group which varied in age from 9.3 to 14.0 to test three hypotheses underlying the use of kinesthetic methods in remedial reading cases.

ROBERTSON, JEAN E. Kindergarten perception training: its effect on first grade reading. In Helen K. Smith (Ed.), *Perception and Reading,* Proceedings of the International Reading Association, *12(4),* 1968, 93-99.
Cites 15 references used as the bases for perception training suggestions for kindergarten and first grade.

ROBINSON, H. ALAN. Reliability of measures related to reading success of average, disadvantaged, and advantaged kindergarten children. *The Reading Teacher,* December 1966, *20,* 203-209.
Investigates reliability of eight instruments designed to identify visual, auditory, or visuo-motor abilities, or to assess reading readiness or general intelligence.

ROBINSON, HELEN M. Perceptual and conceptual style related to reading. In. J. Allen Figurel (Ed.), *Improvement of Reading through Classroom Practice,* International Reading Association Conference Proceedings, *9,* 1964, 26-28.
Considers a number of studies investigating visual perception on primary level through college level.

ROBINSON, HELEN M., et al. Children's perceptual achievement forms: a three year study. *American Journal of Optometry and Archives of American Academy of Optometry,* May 1960, *37,* 223-237.
Reports the results of a study to determine the value of the Children's Perceptual Achievement Forms as a predictor of reading achieve-

ment, using scores on various tests given to those of 87 first-grade pupils in 1956-1957 who remained in school for the 3 years.

RODENBORN, LEO V., JR. The importance of memory and integration factors to oral reading ability. *Journal of Reading Behavior,* Winter 1970-1971, *3(1),* 51-59.
Constructs and administers measures of auditory memory, visual memory, and auditory-visual integration to 180 pupils in grades one to six in order to determine their predictive validity for oral reading achievement.

ROSEN, CARL L. An experimental study of visual perceptual training and reading achievement in first grade. *Perceptual and Motor Skills,* June 1966, *22,* 929-986.
Relates scores on reading readiness, visual perception, and intelligence measures to post-instructional reading achievement scores of 637 pupils in 25 first-grade classrooms, 12 of which received visual perceptual training during scheduled reading periods for 29 days.

ROSEN, CARL L., & OHNMACHT, F. Perception, readiness, and reading achievement in first grade. In Helen K. Smith (Ed.), *Perception and Reading,* Proceedings of the International Reading Association, *12*(4), 1968, 33-39.
Uses factor analysis procedures in analyzing separately by sex scores on readiness, perception, and reading achievement subtests administered to 324 boys and 313 girls.

ROSNER, JEROME. Language arts and arithmetic achievement, and specifically related perceptual skills. *American Educational Research Journal,* Winter 1973, *10,* 59-68.
Compares the auditory visual perceptual skills of 434 first and second graders to their achievement in reading and arithmetic.

ROSNER, JEROME. School achievement as related to IQ and perceptual skills: a comparison of predictors. *Journal of the Optometric Association,* February 1972, *44,* 142-144.
Evaluates use of IQ scores and perceptual skills scores as predictors of achievement of 72 first and second graders.

RUDE, ROBERT T.; NIQUETTE, SHELDON; & FOXGROVER, PHYLLIS. The retention of visual and auditory discrimination reading skills. *The Journal of Educational Research,* January 1975, *68,* 192-196.
Reports results of standardized prereading tests administered to 119 kindergarteners in May and again in September.

RUDNICK, MARK; STERRITT, GRAHAM M.; & FLAX, MORTON. Auditory and visual rhythm perception and reading ability. *Child Development,* June 1967, *38,* 581-587.

Correlates three perceptual tests (auditory, visual, and visual-auditory) with measures of intelligence and reading achievement for 36 third-grade boys of middle class background.

RUPLEY, WILLIAM H.; ASHE, MICHAEL; & BUCKLAND, PEARL. The relation between the discrimination of letter-like forms and word recognition. *Reading World,* December 1979, *19,* 113-123.
Studies the visual discrimination abilities of children who varied in their word recognition ability. First, second, and third-grade pupils in one elementary school were administered the Wide Range Achievement Test (WRAT). On the basis of the WRAT scores, subjects were divided into high, average, and low reading groups, and five boys and five girls were then selected at random at each ability level. Final data were obtained on 28 first graders, 29 second graders, and 30 third graders. Subjects were also given the Otis-Lennon Mental Ability Test — Elementary Level I, and scores were used as a covariate in the analysis. The discrimination task administered required subjects to match a standard artificial grapheme with an identical form when the identical form was placed with a maximum of 12 transformations of the standard. Errors on the task were classified into six categories. The main effect for grade was significant, but neither word recognition skill nor the grade × word recognition skill interaction approached significance. The authors state that the implications of the study are that visual discrimination skills of the type needed to discriminate between single artificial graphemes do not appear to be essential for word recognition.

RUSSELL, DAVID H., & GROFF, PATRICK. Personal factors influencing perception in reading. *Education,* May 1955, *75,* 600-603.
Reviews the results of a series of studies which support the view that the child's perception in reading "is affected by many factors other than the visual, auditory or kinesthetic methods in which he is trained by the teacher."

RUTHERFORD, WILLIAM L. Vision and perception in the reading process. In J. Allen Figurel (Ed.), *Vistas in Reading,* International Reading Association Conference Proceedings, *11(1),* 1966, 503-507.
Recognizes vision and perception as vital factors in the reading process.

RYSTROM, RICHARD. Evaluating letter discrimination problems in the primary grades. *Journal of Reading Behavior,* Fall 1969, *1,* 38-48.
Develops a behavioral definition of letter recognition, presents a test for measuring the extent to which children can recognize letters, and reports data for 93 kindergarteners through third graders using the test.

SABATINO, DAVID A.; SPIDAL, DAVID; & OHRTMAN, WILLIAM. Evaluation of a visual-perceptual training program of word and form constancy. *Psychology in the Schools,* October 1971, *8,* 390-398.
Studies the effects of a visual-perceptual form-constancy training program on the reading performance of 22 children attending a learning disability program and compares their performance with that of a control group of 22.

SAMUELS, S. JAY. Effect of distinctive feature training on paired-associate learning. *Journal of Educational Psychology,* April 1973, *64,* 164-170.
Hypothesizes that visual discrimination training for 90 kindergarten students on noting distinctive features of a stimulus during the perceptual learning phase facilitates S-R hook-up.

SAPHIER, J. D. The relation of perceptual-motor skills to learn ing and school success. *Journal of Learning Disabilities,* No 'ember 1973, *6,* 583-592.
Presents a review of research examining the relationship between measurable perceptual-motor skills in young children and academic success.

SCOTT, R. Perceptual skills, general intellectual ability, race, and later reading achievement. *The Reading Teacher,* 1970, *23,* 660-668.
Reports a series of experiments based on the theory of Piaget and Inhelder of the interaction between perception and language. Subjects were 356 black and white kindergarten children, 151 of whom were tested in reading at third grade.

SCOTT, RALPH. Perceptual readiness as a predictor of success in reading. *The Reading Teacher,* October 1968, *22,* 36-39.
Reports the results of a followup evaluation of 173 kindergarten children's scores on an experimental seriation test and their second-grade reading attainments.

SEATON, HAL W. The effects of a visual perception training program on reading achievement. *Journal of Reading Behavior,* Summer 1977, *9,* 188-192.
Proposes to determine the relative effects of visual perception training on beginning reading with children identified as deficient in visual perception skills. Subjects were randomly selected from 17 grade 1 classrooms in a large suburban school district. The Children's Perceptual Achievement Forms Test was administered during the first month of first grade to 441 children. Children who scored at or below 59 on the test were identified as having a deficiency in visual perceptual skills and were randomly assigned to the Experimental Group or Control Group 1. Children who scored above 75 were randomly selected and assigned to Control Group 2. There were 32 children in each group. Experimental subjects received 37 training

sessions of 20 minutes each over a 12-week period using the Winter Haven Perception Training Program. Teachers were given 14 hours of inservice training in the use of the program. Controls received no special training. Following training, the Word Knowledge, Word Analysis, and Comprehension sections of the Metropolitan Achievement Tests were administered. A significant difference among groups was found for the Word Knowledge subtest only, and the difference favored Control Group 2 over the experimentals. The author questions the value of such training.

SHAPIRO, JON E. The effects of visual discrimination training on reading readiness test performance of impulsive first grade boys. *The Journal of Educational Research,* May/June 1976, *69,* 338-340.

Administers the Matching Familiar Figures (MFF) test to 90 first grade boys to determine their conceptual tempo, and studies the effect of a visual discrimination treatment on boys identified from the test as impulsive. Thirty-two subjects were classified as impulsive and were administered the Gates-MacGinitie Readiness Skills Test (GMRST). Subjects were then randomly assigned to either an experimental or control group. Experimentals met in groups of 4 for 20-minute sessions daily for 20 days and received visual discrimination training. Controls received regular classroom instruction. At the end of the treatment period, subjects were posttested on the GMRST. Experimentals were significantly superior over controls on the composite scores and on 6 of the 8 subtest scores of the GMRST.

SHARAN, SHLOMO, & CALFEE, ROBERT. The relation of auditory, visual and auditory-visual matching to reading performance of Israeli children. *The Journal of Genetic Psychology,* June 1977, *130,* 181-189.

Reports a study in which a variety of visual and auditory matching tasks were administered to 120 second through fourth graders of varying reading ability. Matching tasks were prepared according to the following factors: stimulus type (verbal or nonverbal), modality of the task (visual-visual, auditory-auditory, and auditory-visual), and position of difference (paired stimuli differing in initial, medial, or final position). Verbal tests consisted of pairs of 3-letter words, while nonverbal tests were comprised of dot patterns. Six tests were constructed according to the modality by stimulus type variation. A battery of reading tests was administered to all subjects and consisted of a test of visual memory for words; word, sentence, and syllable reading tests; and a comprehension test of 35 paragraphs of 2 sentences each. Multiple regression analysis revealed that overall matching test scores accounted for 35 percent of the variance in reading scores. All subjects performed virtually perfectly on visual-

visual matching tests. Auditory-auditory matches were more difficult than auditory-visual matches with nonverbal stimuli, while the reverse was true with verbal stimuli.

SHAW, EVA. The effects of attentional focus on graphic discrimination. *The Alberta Journal of Educational Research*, June 1979, *25*, 103-116.
Compares the effectiveness of four methods of training young children in the visual discrimination of letters. The subjects were 132 children between the ages of 4-0 and 4-6 attending day-care centers. Children were randomly assigned to one of four experimental training groups: 1) subjects were to tell if two matching solid black letters were the same, errors were corrected; 2) same as 1, except the letters were in two tones; 3) same stimuli as in 1, but the lines and curves of the letter were described by the examiner; 4) again, the same stimuli as in 1, but the examiner elicited from the subject a verbal description of the lines, curves, and directions of the letters. Performance on three letter matching tests was the dependent variable. Treatment 4, in which the subject was required to describe orally the lines, curves, and direction of the letters, was significantly superior to the other 3 groups in letter matching. These results are used to amend Gough's model of reading.

SHEA, CAROL ANN. Visual discrimination of words and reading readiness. *The Reading Teacher*, January 1968, *21*, 361-367.
Develops a Test of Visual Discrimination of Words using 134 kindergarten children and then uses this test and two other tests as predictors of reading achievement at midyear in first grade for 34 boys and 42 girls.

SILVER, A. A., & HAGIN, ROSA A. Visual perception in children with reading disabilities. In F. A. Young and D. B. Lindsley (Eds.), *Early experience and visual information processing in perceptual and reading disorders*. Washington, D.C.: National Academy of Sciences, 1970, 445-456.
Refers to 36 articles in discussing what visual perceptual defects are associated with delayed acquisiton of reading skills and also what happens to the defects as the child matures.

SMYTHE, P. C.; STENNETT, R. G.; HARDY, MADELINE; & WILSON, H. R. Developmental patterns in elemental reading skills: visual discrimination of primary-type upper-case and lower-case letters. *Journal of Reading Behavior*, Fall 1970-1971, *3(4)*, 6-13.
Employs 200 pupils, kindergarten through grade three, in studying the development of the ability to discriminate upper- and lowercase letters of the alphabet.

SMYTHE, P. C.; STENNETT, R. G.; HARDY, MADELINE; & WILSON, H. R. Developmental patterns in elemental skills: knowledge of upper-case

and lower-case letter names. *Journal of Reading Behavior,* Summer 1970-1971, *3(3),* 24-33.
Assesses the ability of 200 children, kindergarten through grade three, to identify upper and lowercase letter names. Determines the relationship of this knowledge to visual discrimination and notes developmental growth trends.

SNYDER, ROBERT T., & FREUD, SHELDON L. Reading readiness and its relation to maturational unreadiness as measured by the spiral aftereffect and other visual-perceptual techniques. *Perceptual and Motor Skills,* December 1967, *25,* 841-854.
Explores the relationship between success on the Spiral Aftereffect Test, other perceptual tests, and reading readiness tests with 667 first graders.

SOLAN, HAROLD A. Visual processing training with the tachistoscope: a rationale and grade one norms. *Journal of Learning Disabilities,* January 1969, *2,* 30-37.
Proposes to establish a set of expected tachistoscopic responses which will identify children in grades 1, 2, and 3 whose visual sensory maturation is lagging using a percentile scale constructed on the performance of 250 children whose average age was 6 years, 5 months.

SPERLING, GEORGE. Short-term memory, long-term memory, and scanning in the processing of visual information. In F. A. Young & D. B. Lindsley (Eds.), *Early experience and visual information processing in perceptual and reading disorders.* Washington, D. C.: National Academy of Sciences, 1970, 198-215.
Proposes a model of visual-information processing from an array of letters. Information from 18 sources is used in the development of the model.

STAATS, CAROLYN K.; STAATS, ARTHUR W.; & SCHULTZ, RICHARD E. The effects of discrimination pretraining on textual behavior. *Journal of Educational Psychology,* February 1962, *53,* 32-37.
Studies 36 subjects from two kindergartens who were matched on mental age and assigned to one of three discrimination pretraining groups to ascertain effects of this pretraining on textual behavior.

STALLER, JOSHUA, & SEKULER, ROBERT. Children read normal and reversed letters: a simple test of reading skill. *Quarterly Journal of Experimental Psychology,* November 1975, *27,* 539-550.
Investigates letter recognition latencies with 72 third, fifth, and seventh graders judged above or below average in reading achievement. Letters were presented in 2 conditions: normal orientation and left-right mirror image orientation. The ratio of naming time on normal letters to naming time on mirror image letters was calculated

for each subject. Good readers had lower ratios than poor readers due primarily to the faster naming of normal letters among good readers. Good and poor readers named mirror image letters at similar speeds. Results are discussed with reference to possible memory deficits and/or increased skill in processing peripheral information.

STANOVICH, KEITH E.; WEST, RICHARD F.; & POLLAK, DENISE. The effect of orthographic structure on word recognition in a visual search task. *Journal of Experimental Child Psychology,* August 1978, *26,* 137-146.
Investigates the visual search performance of twenty-four third graders, twenty-four sixth graders, and twenty-four college students on tasks of identifying one word; a semantic category; or 3 words in lists of words, nonwords and pseudowords. Influence of orthographic structure was significant in searching for categories and three word targets. Use of orthographic structure to facilitate search did not increase with age of these subjects.

STAYTON, SAMUEL, & FULLER, RENEE. Reading level of retardates related to visual and auditory memory, and to paired-associate learning. *Training School Bulletin,* February 1974, *70,* 202-207.
Reports the correlations between reading scores and 3 tasks including paired-associate, visual retention, and auditory retention. Subjects were 180 residents and 12 outpatients at an institution for the retarded.

STEEN, MARCIA, & SOWELL, VIRGINIA. Effects of training in directionality on reversals in reading and writing. *Perceptual and Motor Skills,* February 1980, *50,* 219-224.
Conducts a study to determine the effects of training in directionality on word and letter reversals. Subjects were 13 boys and 11 girls attending a summer school remedial program who demonstrated a tendency to reverse letters or words on a pretest constructed by the authors. The control group received the usual remedial program plus an additional 15 minutes of remedial instruction. The experimental group received the usual remedial instruction plus 15 minutes of training in directionality. The program lasted four weeks. The pretest was used as the posttest. There were no significant differences between the two groups.

STERRITT, GRAHAM M.; MARTIN, VIRGINIA E.; & RUDNICK, MARK. The role of visual perception: sequential pattern perception and reading. In G. D. Spache (Ed.), *Reading Disability and Perception,* International Reading Association Conference Proceedings, *13,* 1969, 61-71.
Attempts to define the role of various kinds of sequence in perceptual abilities as related to the development of reading skills using 40

middle-class Caucasian third graders (20 boys and 20 girls) whose mean age was 109 months.

STERRITT, GRAHAM M., & RUDNICK, MARK. Auditory and visual rhythm perception in relation to reading ability in fourth grade boys. *Perceptual and Motor Skills,* June 1966, *22,* 859-864.
Studies relationships among mean scores of 36 boys on measures of intelligence, reading comprehension, and tests of visual, auditory, and visual-auditory perception.

SUPER, SELWYN. Spatial perception of language symbols and a description of a test designed to assess this function. *American Journal of Optometry and Archives of American Academy of Optometry,* June 1969, *46,* 426-433.
Describes a test for the selection of letter recognition as part of the assessment of a child's reading ability using a random sample of 60 good and poor achievers from a normal school, and 40 children of average or above intelligence from a special school for learning difficulties in grades 1 through 6.

SWANSON, LEE. Verbal encoding effects on the visual short-term memory of learning disabled and normal readers. *Journal of Educational Psychology,* August 1978, *70,* 530-544.
Investigates the hypothesis that the reading difficulties of learning disabled children are attributable to deficiencies in verbal encoding. Subjects were 30 learning disabled and 30 normal readers averaging in age about 9-5. Learning disabled subjects scored below the 30th percentile on the Wide Range Achievement Test and two reading subtests of the Peabody Individual Achievement Test. Normal readers scored at grade level or above. Names were assigned that reflected the experimenter's impressions of the shapes. Half of each group of children learned the names of the six shapes, while the other half was given practice in discriminating top and bottom contours. The experimental task was a probe-type serial memory task. The named condition was superior for normal readers. No difference was found in recall of non-verbal (unnamed) stimuli between normal and learning disabled children. The author suggests that reading deficits in learning disabled children are related to verbal encoding limitations, not to deficiencies of visual memory, as suggested by the perceptual deficit hypothesis.

THORSON, GARY. An alternative for judging confusability of visual letters. *Perceptual and Motor Skills,* February 1976, *42,* 116-118.
Tabulates numerical values of gross overlap of distinctive features of the 26 capital letters, supported by a previous study of reaction time when judging letter pairs.

TIMKO, HENRY G. Configuration as a cue in the word recognition of beginning readers. *Journal of Experimental Education,* 1970, *39,* 68-69.

Compares the relative saliency of identical letters and geometric shapes, as well as the main effect of these variables and their interactions on the word recognition ability of 40 first-grade children.

TIMKO, HENRY G. Effects of discrimination training mode and letter similarity on paired-associate learning. *The Journal of Educational Research,* October 1974, *68,* 71-72.

Analyzes relationships among simultaneous and successive presentation of confusable and distinctive letters in terms of trials to criterion and transfer of training to words. Subjects were 40 first graders.

TIMKO, HENRY G. Letter position in trigram discrimination by beginning readers. *Perceptual and Motor Skills,* August 1972, *35,* 153-154.

Reports the effect that change in letter position has on the tendency of 31 first graders to use the outer letters of trigrams more often than medial ones. The tests were 40 matching-to-sample discrimination.

TORGESEN, JOSEPH K.; BOWEN, CHARLES; & IVEY, CHARLES. Task structure versus modality of presentation: a study of the construct validity of the visual-aural digit span test. *Journal of Educational Psychology,* August 1978, *70,* 451-456.

Attempts to determine which of two variables, task structure or modality of presentation, is most important in accounting for performance differences between good and poor readers on the Visual-Aural Digit Span Test (VADS). Subjects were 60 fourth-grade boys, all of whom scored between 90 and 120 on the Institute for Personality and Ability Testing Culture Fair Intelligence Test (IPAT) and who were categorized as good or poor readers. Poor readers were boys who scored 3.5 or below on the Wide Range Achievement Test (WRAT) and were identified by their teachers as having problems in reading. The mean reading grade level for poor readers on the WRAT was 2.5; for good readers, it was 6.3. Subjects were administered four subtests from the VADS plus two tasks involving visual/sequential presentation that had been developed specifically for the study. Differences between the groups were significant only for the Visual-Oral and Visual-Written subtests even though these two tasks were easiest for both groups. Thus it was concluded that task structure was a more potent variable in determining individual differences than was modality of presentation.

TOWNER, JOHN C., & EVANS, HOWARD M. The effect of three-dimensional stimuli versus two-dimensional stimuli on visual form discrimination. *Journal of Reading Behavior,* December 1974, *6,* 395-402.

Compares the effects of distinctive feature training using 2-dimensional letter-like forms with distinctive feature training using 3-dimensional letter-like forms. Forty randomly selected kindergarten children were randomly assigned to one of the 2 conditions. Both groups were presented with a transfer task involving visual discrimination among 2-dimensional letter-like forms. Results favored the 3-dimensional training group.

TURAIDS, DAINIS; WEPMAN, JOSEPH M.; & MORENCY, ANNE. A perceptual test battery: development and standardization. *The Elementary School Journal,* April 1972, *72,* 351-361.

Describes the development and standardization of a test battery exploring the auditory and visual perceptual processing abilities of children. The sample consisted of 1,008 children, ages 5-8, who were individually tested.

VANDEVER, THOMAS R., & NEVILLE, DONALD D. Letter cues versus configuration cues as aids to word recognition in retarded and non-retarded children. *American Journal of Mental Deficiency,* September 1974, *79,* 210-213.

Uses a contrived orthography to investigate learning speed and retention in 59 lower to lower middleclass, mentally retarded children (with WISC IQs less than 85) and 53 middleclass non-mentally retarded first and second graders randomly assigned to one of 3 conditions (outline, contrast, letter cue).

VAN DE VOORT, LEWIS, & SENF, GERALD M. Audiovisual integration in retarded readers. *Journal of Learning Disabilities,* March 1973, *6,* 170-179.

Explores basic visual and auditory abilities which could account for auditory-visual integration problems by comparing 16 retarded with 16 normal readers.

VELLUTINO, FRANK R.; PRUZEK, ROBERT M.; STEGER, JOSEPH A.; & MESHOULAM, URIEL. Immediate visual recall in poor and normal readers as a function of orthographic-linguistic familiarity. *Cortex,* December 1973, *9,* 370-386.

Attempts to determine the relative influence of spatial and other perceptual difficulties on the reading ability of 63 fourth through sixth graders defined as normal or poor readers.

VELLUTINO, FRANK R.; STEGER, JOSEPH A.; KAMAN, MITCHELL; & DESETTO, LOUIS. Visual form perception in deficient and normal readers as a function of age and orthographic-linguistic familiarity. *Cortex,* March 1975, *11,* 22-30.

Compares reproductions from memory of briefly presented Hebrew words by 22 poor and 44 normal readers in second and fourth grades. Each grade level contained equal numbers of poor and normal readers unfamiliar with Hebrew and normal readers learning Hebrew.

VELLUTINO, FRANK R.; STEGER, JOSEPH A.; & PRUZEK, ROBERT M. Inter- vs. intransensory deficit in paired associate learning in poor and normal readers. *Canadian Journal of Behavior Science,* April 1973, *5,* 111-123.
Compares good and poor readers in 2 groups of 30 fourth and sixth graders on visual-visual and visual-auditory paired associate tasks.

VERNON, M. D. *Backwardness in reading: a study of its nature and origin.* Cambridge: The University Press, 1958.
Summarizes experimental and clinical studies of those who for some reason or other are unable to master the simple mechanics of reading, using the following headings: visual perception, auditory perception, innate factors, acquired defects, and environmental factors.

VERNON, M. D. The perceptual process in reading. *The Reading Teacher,* October 1959, *13,* 2-8.
Summarizes evidence from 22 studies relating to nature of the perceptual process in reading and how words are perceived.

VERNON, M. D. Ten more important sources of information on visual perception in relation to reading. *The Reading Teacher,* November 1966, *20,* 134-135.
Summarizes 10 selected studies on visual perception and reading.

VERNON, MAGDALEN D. *Visual perception and its relation to reading: an annotated bibliography.* Newark, Delaware: International Reading Association, 1966.
Abstracts 55 studies under four headings: perception of shape by young children; perception of words by children; perception in backward readers; and perception of shapes, letters, and words by adults.

WALLBROWN, JANE D.; WALLBROWN, FRED H.; & ENGIN, ANN W. The relative importance of mental age and selected assessors of auditory and visual perception in the Metropolitan Readiness Test. *Psychology in the Schools,* April 1974, *11,* 136-143.
Utilizes 215 kindergarteners in assessing the importance of auditory, visual and mental-age components in total scores on a standardized reading readiness test.

WALLBROWN, JANE D.; WALLBROWN, FRED H.; ENGIN, ANN W.; & BLAHA, JOHN. The prediction of first grade reading achievement with selected perceptual-cognitive tests. *Psychology in the Schools,* April 1975, *12,* 140-149.

Analyzes regression of first grade reading achievement on 10 predictor variables assessed in kindergarten, including IQ, perceptual abilities, and language comprehension. Subjects were a more or less stratified random sample of 100 children.

WALTERS, C. ETTA. Reading ability and visual-motor function in second
grade children. *Perceptual and Motor Skills*, December 1961, *13*, 370.

Makes a comparison of performance on the Memory-for-Designs Test and a balance test between grade 2 pupils who read at average or above and those who read below average.

WALTERS, RICHARD H., & KOSOWSKI, IRENE. Symbolic learning and reading retardation. *Journal of Consulting Psychology*, February 1963, *27*, 75-82.

Compares 24 each of advanced, average, and retarded readers in grades 6 to 8 on their ability to learn through visual and auditory stimuli in conjunction with the different reading levels, and assesses the effects of transfer from one sense modality to another.

WARREN, DAVID H.; ANOOSHIAN, LINDA J.; & WIDAWSKI, MEL H. Measures of visual-auditory integration and their relations to reading achievement in early grades. *Perceptual and Motor Skills*, October 1975, *41*, 615-630.

Studies the relationship between reading achievement and several visual-auditory integration tasks with more than 300 first through third graders. Subjects were assessed for reading achievement with the Cooperative Primary Test. Subjects were also given 4 visual-auditory integration tasks: 1) reaction time, tested by interspersed light and buzzer stimuli to which subjects responded by pressing a button; 2) bisensory memory, tested by 3 stimulus pairs of simultaneously presented visual and auditory digits where subjects were to recall pair members; 3) pattern-matching, tested by temporal patterns of interspersed visual and auditory elements that subjects were required to recall; and 4) auditory distraction, tested as performance on a visual-spatial relations test with and without auditory distraction. Results indicated that there were separate integrative abilities and that several of the integrative measures were correlated with reading independently of the other measures; additionally, it was shown that some of the integrative measures accounted for significant reading variance beyond that usually accounted for by intelligence tests.

WAUGH, RUTH, & WATSON, ZANA. Visual perception and reading.
*Education*, 1970, *91*, 181-184.

Surveys the literature relative to visual perception and reading to ascertain if visual perception is significantly related to reading achievement, and if visual perception training improves reading ability.

WEINER, PAUL S. A revision of the Chicago Test of Visual Discrimination. *Elementary School Journal,* April 1968, *68,* 373-380.

Reports on the standardization of the extended form of the Chicago Test of Visual Discrimination using 90 6-, 7-, and 8-year-olds as the extended form was correlated with intellectual functioning, visual motor ability, and school achievement (including reading) for 201 7- and 8-year-olds.

WEINER, PAUL S.; WEPMAN, JOSEPH M.; & MORENCY, ANNE S. A test of visual discrimination. *Elementary School Journal,* March 1965, *65,* 330-337.

Describes the development and standardization of the Chicago Test of Visual Discrimination and compares the performances of 28 good readers and 28 poor readers at the fourth-grade level on this test as well as on the Wepman Auditory Discrimination Test.

WHEELOCK, WARREN H. An investigation of visual discrimination training for beginning readers. In Helen K. Smith (Ed.), *Perception and Reading,* Proceedings of the International Reading Association, 12(4), 1968, 101-105.

Studies the effect of training on the instant letter recognition and visual discrimination ability of 45 experimental kindergarten children as compared to 45 control children.

WHEELOCK, WARREN H., & SILVAROLI, NICHOLAS M. Investigation of visual discrimination training for beginning readers. *Journal of Typographic Research,* April 1967, *1,* 147-156.

Compares visual discrimination ability for 45 experimental kindergartners who were trained to make instant responses of recognition to the capital letters of the alphabet with 45 control subjects receiving no training.

WHISLER, NANCY G. Visual memory training and its effects on visual discrimination skill and total reading ability. *Elementary English,* September 1973, *50,* 936-938.

Tests the null hypothesis that there is no significant difference in visual discrimination skill or total reading ability for 152 first graders who partook in a visual memory program, compared to 143 controls.

WHISLER, NANCY G. Visual-memory training in first grade: effects on visual discrimination and reading ability. *The Elementary School Journal,* October 1974, *75,* 51-54.

Uses analysis of covariance to compare reading achievement and visual skills of 152 first graders who received 15 weeks of visual memory training in addition to their regular instruction with achievement of 143 children who had received only basal instruction.

WIEDERHOLT, J. LEE, & HAMMILL, DONALD D. Use of the Frostig-Horne Visual Perception Program in the urban school. *Psychology in the Schools,* July 1971, *8,* 268-274.
Examines the effect on reading of the Frostig training program with 170 kindergarten and first-grade subjects.

WILHELM, ROWENA. Diagnostic value of test score differentials found between measures of visual and auditory memory in severely disabled readers. *Academic Therapy Quarterly,* Fall 1966, *2,* 42-44, 58.
Compares scores in visual memory (Knox Cube Test) and auditory memory (Digit Span Test of the Wechsler Intelligence Scale for Children) for severely retarded readers and relates the differential to muscular tension, age, sex, and other variables.

WILLIAMS, JOANNA P. Some experiments on visual and aural word recognition. In Frank P. Greene (Ed.), Reading: the right to participate. *Twentieth Yearbook of the National Reading Conference,* 1971, 78-84.
Reports several laboratory experiments on visual and aural word recognition using kindergartners, first graders and adults as subjects.

WILLIAMS, JOANNA P. Training kindergarten children to discriminate letter-like forms. *American Educational Research Journal,* November 1969, *6,* 501-514.
Develops two experiments to determine the most effective of three training methods used to develop visual discrimination of forms resembling letters by 64 kindergarten children.

WILLIAMS, JOANNA P.; BLUMBERG, ELLEN L.; & WILLIAMS, D. V. Cues used in visual word recognition. *Journal of Educational Psychology,* 1970, *61,* 310-315.
Determines the characteristics of words discriminated by 17 kindergarten children, 15 first graders, and 32 college students using a delayed matching-to-sample technique.

WILSON, ROSE; PARKER, TIMOTHY; STEVENSON, HAROLD W.; & WILKINSON, ALEX. Perceptual discrimination as a predictor of achievement in reading and arithmetic. *Journal of Educational Psychology,* April 1979, *71,* 220-225.
Examines perceptual discrimination of letterlike forms among 410 prekindergarten children and its relationship to reading achievement. Subjects were administered a battery of perceptual discrimination tasks using letterlike forms and their transformations. Subjects were tested further at grades 1, 2, and 3 with the Wide Range

Achievement Test. The magnitude of the relation to subsequent achievement in reading differed for different transformations, depending upon the difficulty of a transformation. More easily discriminated transformations were associated with higher correlations. The patterns of relation were similar for reading and arithmetic, suggesting that the perceptual discrimination test measured nonperceptual abilities related to early school achievement.

YUSSEN, STEVEN R. The effects of verbal and visual highlighting of dimensions on discrimination learning by preschoolers and second graders. *Child Development,* September 1972, *43,* 921-929.

Describes discrimination training given 60 preschoolers and 60 second graders. Training involved 2 simultaneously presented forms under different conditions of visual and verbal highlighting of dimensions. A transfer problem was then presented.

0112005